Praise for

Every Woman a T~~heologian~~

"*This* is the book we've been waiting for Phylicia Masonheimer to write for years! She has served as the stalwart, trusted, and wise guide for a generation of women who have come to understand that they are, indeed, theologians. And now, she pulls her astute observations and teachings into a single, stellar book pointing the way toward an intimacy with God, where we love him not only with our hearts, but with our minds as well."

—Jennifer Dukes Lee, author of *Growing Slow* and *It's All Under Control*

"In an age obsessed with fads and fleeting moments, Phylicia rises above the fray and presents us a with something ultimate and timeless: a book that helps us understand and faithfully follow God. Her systematic approach to theology is true to her style—easy to understand but simultaneously full of understanding. Her wise words cut through the confusion surrounding theology and give us the gift of clarity. *Every Woman a Theologian* is a resource for any woman (or man!) ready to discover just how essential theology is to a vibrant faith. Highly recommended!"

—Dr. Steve Bezner, senior pastor, Houston Northwest Church

"With biblical maturity and clarity, Phylicia has given us a primer for understanding theological truths in ways that cause us to know, love, and enjoy God more. Fearlessly breaking down complicated ideas and fairly offering various interpretations, *Every Woman A Theologian* is practical, applicable, and helpful."

—Laura Wifler, author, podcaster, and co-founder of Risen Motherhood

"I read Phylicia's words, and I want to pick up my Bible — she makes me want to know Him in the pages of His Word. Her book is a gift for this current hour, yet timeless in its message."

—Sara Hagerty, bestselling author of *Unseen: The Gift of Being Hidden in a World that Loves to be Noticed* and *Adore*

"*Every Woman a Theologian* is both winsome and thorough. Phylicia Masonheimer seamlessly weaves theological depth, historical perspective, and real life application into one really superb volume. I strongly recommend this book to anyone seeking a deeper understanding of historic Christian theology on a level that is accessible to all, and in a tone that manages to be both winsome and sophisticated."

—RYAN COATNEY, FOUNDER OF CROSS FORMED KIDS AND
FOUNDING PASTOR OF GRACE STORY CHURCH

"If theology intimidates you but you wish you had better answers to life's biggest questions, *Every Woman a Theologian* will help you bridge the gap between devotional books and academic commentaries. Find in Phylicia a trustworthy friend who will help you both understand what you believe and grow to more deeply love the One in whom we believe."

— ASHERITAH CIUCIU, BESTSELLING AUTHOR AND
HOST OF THE PRAYERS OF REST PODCAST

Every
Woman
a
Theologian

KNOW WHAT YOU BELIEVE.

LIVE IT CONFIDENTLY.

COMMUNICATE IT GRACIOUSLY.

PHYLICIA MASONHEIMER

W PUBLISHING GROUP

AN IMPRINT OF THOMAS NELSON

Every Woman a Theologian

© 2023 Phylicia Masonheimer

All rights reserved. No portion of this book may be reproduced, stored in a retrieval system, or transmitted in any form or by any means—electronic, mechanical, photocopy, recording, scanning, or other—except for brief quotations in critical reviews or articles, without the prior written permission of the publisher.

Published in Nashville, Tennessee, by W Publishing, an imprint of Thomas Nelson.

Thomas Nelson titles may be purchased in bulk for educational, business, fund-raising, or sales promotional use. For information, please email SpecialMarkets@ThomasNelson.com. Any internet addresses, phone numbers, or company or product information printed in this book are offered as a resource and are not intended in any way to be or to imply an endorsement by Thomas Nelson, nor does Thomas Nelson vouch for the existence, content, or services of these sites, phone numbers, companies, or products beyond the life of this book.

Unless otherwise noted, Scripture quotations are taken from the Holy Bible, New International Version®, NIV®. Copyright © 1973, 1978, 1984, 2011 by Biblica, Inc.® Used by permission of Zondervan. All rights reserved worldwide. www.zondervan.com. The "NIV" and "New International Version" are trademarks registered in the United States Patent and Trademark Office by Biblica, Inc.®

Scripture quotations marked AMP are taken from the Amplified® Bible (AMP). Copyright © 2015 by The Lockman Foundation. Used by permission. www.Lockman.org.

Scripture quotations marked ESV are taken from the ESV® Bible (The Holy Bible, English Standard Version®). Copyright © 2001 by Crossway, a publishing ministry of Good News Publishers. Used by permission. All rights reserved.

Scripture quotations marked GNT are taken from the Good News Translation in Today's English Version—Second Edition. Copyright © 1992 by American Bible Society. Used by permission.

Scripture quotations marked HCSB are taken from the Holman Christian Standard Bible®. Copyright © 1999, 2000, 2002, 2003, 2009 by Holman Bible Publishers. Used by permission. HCSB® is a federally registered trademark of Holman Bible Publishers.

Scripture quotations marked NKJV are taken from the New King James Version®. Copyright © 1982 by Thomas Nelson. Used by permission. All rights reserved.

Scripture quotations marked NRSV are taken from the New Revised Standard Version, Updated Edition. Copyright © 2021 National Council of Churches of Christ in the United States of America. Used by permission. All rights reserved worldwide.

ISBN 978-0-7852-9225-8 (audiobook)
ISBN 978-0-7852-9224-1 (eBook)
ISBN 978-0-7852-9222-7 (HC)
ISBN 978-0-7852-9223-4 (SC)

Library of Congress Control Number: 2022048802

Printed in the United States of America
23 24 25 26 27 LBC 5 4 3 2 1

To Josh

Yours is the knock at the office door, the hand
holding coffee, holding me; you are the iron
I am sharpened upon, sparks and fire flying.
We fight, we work, we bend, we try again.
And when it all becomes too much,
you approve what others could not,
strengthen me again to standing,
and I carry on one more day
because of you.

Contents

Contents

Introduction

On a Tuesday, in a brick café in Virginia, theology became essential.

I should not say *became*; rather, theology revealed itself as essential as it has always been. It became essential *for me*.

I was a young mom in my midtwenties reconnecting with an old friend from high school. My friend and I were sipping coffee, talking about the gray weather outside, warmer places, and the intersection of politics and religion (just as Emily Post advises *not* to do). These discussions were not new for us; I am a Christian and she was, at the time, exploring many different religions after having left Christianity behind. Our coffee dates covered incredible philosophical ground, and we sometimes discussed our differing views. We knew we didn't agree, but we weren't particularly direct about it.

Until that Tuesday.

I don't know how the conversation turned from the outdoor temperature to Jesus, but it did—as abruptly as a winter squall.

"I definitely admire Jesus," my friend confessed. "I just think God lets us come to Him in a variety of ways. We're all on the path to Him; it just looks different—Buddhists, Hindus, Muslims, Christians. We're all just finding our way."

I took another drink of my coffee. "What makes you arrive at that conclusion?"

"I just don't think Jesus would have a problem with all these other people finding their way. Like, they're seeking too. Just because it looks different doesn't make it invalid."

"Can I share something?" I asked, setting down my mug.

"Sure."

"I definitely agree that people are seeking; they're looking for answers. They believe there is something greater out there, and they want to attach themselves to that purpose. But, something to consider: Jesus didn't allow for many paths to God."

She raised an eyebrow. "What do you mean?"

"Let's start with how we know who Jesus is. Most of our information is from the Gospels—Matthew, Mark, Luke, and John. All the things we like about Jesus are in there: His love, healings, resistance to power structures, sacrifice. But that's also where we see Jesus say things that make it clear He didn't think there was more than one way to God."

"Like what?"

"In John 14, He says He is the way, truth, and life. He even goes on to say no one can access God unless it's through Him. He says a similar thing in Matthew 11." I adjusted my coffee mug. "I guess what I am saying is: I like your theory, I really do. But Jesus didn't allow for it. So I respect that you admire Jesus, but if you admire Him, you have to take into account everything He said about Himself. He *made* Christianity exclusive."

"I've never heard it explained that way." My friend tapped her coffee cup and narrowed her eyes. "I'll have to think about it."

On a Tuesday, in a brick café in Virginia, theology was essential.

And today, wherever you are in the world, it is essential as well.

We think of theology—the study of the nature of God and His truth—as the stuff of C. S. Lewis; we picture it swirling with pipe smoke and stacked with leather-bound books. We think it's for people with seminary degrees, and it seems irrelevant to the rest of us. Perhaps we think it especially irrelevant to those of us in "normal" jobs and lives: those commuting to work wearing the company polo shirt; those wiping toddler noses and bottoms; those taking care of aging parents. What does theology have to do with *us*?

It has everything to do with you, my friend. And just as theology became essential to me, one day it will become essential to you. It probably already has.

For example, have you ever:

- been asked a tough question about the Bible's trustworthiness and found yourself searching for words?
- attempted to comfort a grieving friend and found yourself struggling to explain how God can be both all-powerful and all-good?
- tried to explain the gospel to an unbelieving friend but couldn't get much further than "ask Jesus into your heart"?
- avoided tough questions about your faith because it's too much work, or you're scared, or you just don't want to know?

If you answered yes to any of these questions, theology has already proved itself essential to your life—you just didn't have the words for it. All the situations I've framed demand that Christian theology provide an answer, and it does.

However, theology doesn't just provide intellectual satisfaction. It also provides *direction*. Like my friend noted, people of all religions are seeking answers. They are seeking God. The world's religions, and even the religion of self, whose followers

THEOLOGY: *the study of the nature of God and His truth*

we call religious "nones," are an attempt to secure purpose and identity, to root oneself in service of something.

C. S. Lewis called this attempt to find happiness and purpose the root of "all that we call human history—money, poverty, ambition, war, prostitution, classes, empires, slavery—the long terrible story of man trying to find something other than God which will make him happy."[1]

Most people want to be happy. The pursuit of happiness is not just a right written into the United States' Declaration of Independence—it's a desire of the human heart. We want to know who we are and where we're going, and we want to be at peace with our world. Therefore happiness is bound up in both purpose and identity.

These pursuits beget deeper theological questions: Who made humans? If God, what was His purpose in making them? What does that say about human identity? How does this change how we live? Like Lewis indicated, people are pursuing happiness apart from their Creator. Theology lays a foundation for answering the tough questions of these same people tired of the "long terrible story" hunting for a God-less happiness.

If you're a Christian, you hold the key to a *God-based* happiness. You hold knowledge that leads to peace and purpose because it leads to Christ. When your average Tuesday comes, will you be ready? Can you "give an answer . . . for the hope that you have . . . with gentleness and respect" (1 Peter 3:15)? Do you know what you believe and why you believe it?

If the answer is no, you're in the right place! I have spent the last six years teaching women how to own their faith, understand basic Christian doctrine, and grow closer to Jesus in the process. This book is the product of that work, and it is my joy to walk alongside you as you are equipped to not just know *about* God but also to know Him intimately, sweetly, and honestly through the study of His character.

The emphasis on intimacy is important here. Too often, studying theology turns the Person of God into the "theory of God." We speculate about Him as if He were a specimen in a petri dish. We hypothesize and analyze and cease to *recognize* that the power of Christianity, the transforming element, is not just in philosophy and reason, though both are honored by our faith. No—Christianity is a personal *transformation*, one that cannot be forced into existence by knowledge alone.

Theology without intimacy is a hollow thing, neither relevant nor compelling. No unbelieving person wants it, and they shouldn't, because it isn't Christianity. Pursue theology to pursue God's heart, and you will be surprised to find that doctrine leads to devotion. (If you find this improbable, consider the encouragement of C. S. Lewis again: "I believe that many who find that nothing happens when they sit down, or kneel down, to a book of devotion, would find that the heart sings unbidden when they are working their way through a tough bit of theology."[2])

Let's go back to that Virginia coffee shop. My friend didn't become a Christian that day. In fact, as far as I know, she never did. The point of our conversation wasn't to push her to a decision; it wasn't for me to change her view. What happened that day was an example of how theology, when rightly understood and pursued, *directly applies to real life.* And if we define theology as the study of God and His truth, then every single Christian should be a theologian! Understanding what we believe and explaining it graciously does not guarantee that our family, friends, and coworkers will follow Jesus. But it equips us to have those conversations and introduce them to His heart.

To become "theologians," we have to shed the academic overtones we've attached to the idea (certainly, there are truly academic theologians, but for the sake of my purpose here we will call them "scholars"). Before theology became an academic pursuit, it was the foundation for a living, active faith in Jesus—and it still is today. Faith is not just a feeling; it requires an engaged mind.

A few years ago I received an email from a young stay-at-home mother with children under the age of four. "At first, your encouragement to study theology felt really irrelevant to me," she wrote. "But eventually I decided to begin. I feel like my faith is alive again. I feel challenged in ways I haven't in years. Thank you for showing me that even a mom who will never go to seminary can know the Bible for herself." Her message brought tears to my eyes. This young mom was realizing the fruit of an engaged Christian mind.

The idea that faith and reason, or intimacy and logic, are on two ends of the Christian spectrum (or are not found within the Christian spectrum at all) is not found in Scripture and is *definitely* not found in the history of the Christian church. The Bible is theology and reason unified, and it demands study and intellectual pursuit—not so we can prove ourselves or because God likes to play games but because God made us *thinking people*. He imparted to us the gift of a reasonable mind, and He expects us to use it.

Christ does not require us to blindly believe. Faith is, after all, only as good as the thing we put our faith in. To believe in God we must first understand *who it is* we are trusting. Christianity is a reasoned faith, and this employment of the mind is how Christianity became a springboard for scientific, philosophical, and logical exploration.[3]

It used to be that religion and reason were not seen as opposites but as complements. Until the 1890s, philosophers were often trained as ministers and theologians, and theological seminaries were the center of philosophical thought.[4] After the Protestant church broke away from the Roman Catholic Church in the 1500s, the subsequent reformation-turned-church split led to many changes in the church landscape, many of which were necessary and good. Some of them encouraged the scientific and philosophical advancements we've seen so far. But one of the long-term impacts of the Reformation was a rejection of church history, liturgy, and tradition. Over time, Christians became forgetful of their shared legacy.

They became more and more individualistic and, in some denominations, humanistic. This was helpful to science but forgetful of Scripture.

Today many Christians follow a humanistic trend by separating what is spiritual from what is logical. They fail to combine the two, instead separating them into completely isolated pursuits. This is the influence of humanism, not a reflection of Scripture's teaching on the mind.

HUMANISM: *a worldview focused on the rational and material rather than the divine or supernatural.*

Every weekday when I was a kid, my mom gathered my siblings and me in the living room for our homeschool routine. As bread baked in the oven, filling the air with the scent of yeast and flour, we rehearsed poems, scientific facts, literary pursuits, and Bible verses. The verses my mom had us memorize are still with me today.

Maybe you memorized verses in Sunday school and got an award for most verses committed to memory (if so, I'm impressed!). One of the verses many of us know is Deuteronomy 6:5: "You shall love the LORD your God with all your heart, with all your soul, and with all your strength" (NKJV). The Gospels (all except John) record a story where Jesus talked about this command. A Jewish teacher of the law asked Jesus which command was the greatest.

The accounts differ a little on the details. In Matthew, Jesus' answer is recorded as, "Love the Lord your God with all your heart and with all your soul and *with all your mind*" (22:37, emphasis added). In Luke, Jesus asked the *teacher* to state the command and the teacher responded, "Love the Lord your God with all your heart and with all your soul and with all your strength and *with all your mind*" (10:27, emphasis added). In Mark, Jesus responded, "Love the Lord your God with all your heart and with all your soul and *with all your mind* and with all your strength" (12:30, emphasis added).

We may find it curious that Jesus added "with all your mind" to the original command. The Greek word used here is *dianoia*, which means understanding, comprehending, or desiring. To love God with our minds is to be loyal to the Lord with our attention, seeking to understand, comprehend, and desire Him.

I love that Jesus wants us to engage our minds with Him. He knows we desire to be challenged! But this doesn't mean we have to spend our days wrestling with thousand-page commentaries from two hundred years ago (unless that's your jam, like it is mine!). It means that clear teaching on the nature of God, the nature of sin, humanity, gender, biblical trustworthiness, and church is vital to the average Christian person. And as our culture becomes more post-Christian (the percentage of American adults who identify as "Christian" is down twelve points in the last decade[5]), apathy is not the answer. A biblical, historical, Christian theology is the key to discerning truth and sharing it with others in an understandable way.

If this feels intimidating, that's okay. It's one reason I wrote this book. If you're new to Christ, or if you've been a Christian but were never encouraged to engage your mind *and* heart in your faith, this can feel like an uphill journey. I'm here to bridge the gap between your usual devotional books and academic theological tomes. As we journey together in this book, I want you to come away with:

- an understanding of what the gospel really is and how it applies to life;
- confidence in your faith and worldview;
- tools to steward difficult questions and doubts; and
- a renewed desire to know God personally and intimately!

We won't cover all the nuanced angles of each topic we discuss in the following pages, but you'll get a general overview to begin your study. And I hope, as you read, you'll have questions and ideas sparking in that beautiful brain of yours—the kinds of questions you can discuss with God in prayer, with friends over coffee, and with people at your church.

I hope I've convinced you that theology is not relegated to damp libraries and ancient books. It's as alive as the God who's at the center of it. It's all around you, every day, in the questions of your coworkers and the conversations with your cousin and the skepticism of your friend. It filters our inner dialogues and doubts. Its current runs through every political debate, every moral judgment, every new idea. Theology is essential because it touches every single area of life.

Are you ready? I hope so! Every woman is a theologian, including you.

A REASONED FAITH: THOMAS AQUINAS

Can the existence of God be established by reason, even in an unbelieving mind? Thomas Aquinas thought so. This medieval scholar believed reason and faith were two ways of knowing God's reality. Reason reveals God in the world, and faith reveals the unique answer to the world's problems: Christ. Aquinas fought for a faith made compatible with reason rather than competing with reason. He believed "reason had a divine right to feed upon facts," and that it is "the business of faith to digest the strong meat of the toughest and most practical of pagan philosophies."[6] His work laid a foundation for the sciences and for future theological exploration.

Bibliology: The Very Breath of God

THE DOCTRINE OF SCRIPTURE

W ill you hang this for me?" I asked my husband, Josh.

"Sure," he replied. We'd been gifted a five-foot "ruler" to mark family height on the wall. It was one of those Hobby Lobby decor pieces thirty-year-old women like me tend to collect. Josh took the dark piece of wood, tucking his pencil behind his ear. The girls watched with saucer eyes, excited by the prospect of seeing their growth.

Minutes later the ruler was on the wall—but something about it was odd. Too high? Too low? Too far to the left? I couldn't quite put a finger on it. *Probably just seeing things*, I shrugged.

We left the ruler on the wall for a few weeks; weeks became months. One day, as the snow fell and blustered around the farmhouse walls, our house was filled with people—people stuffed into the kitchen, stuffed with winter food.

"There is *no* way I'm this tall!" laughed one of our guests. She backed up to the ruler, her husband measuring with his hand. At five foot two, she should have just crested the top; instead, the ruler said she was nearly six feet! The problem dawned on us, and the farmhouse guests laughed: we'd hung the ruler a foot too low. The girls, the guests—we all had grown twelve inches!

When we use a ruler incorrectly, the measurement will inevitably be off. My dad is a home builder. Can you imagine if his ruler was "off"? Entire houses would be unstable! This is dangerous in life, but what about in morality? What is the standard for determining good and evil? This age-old question leaps the confines of theology. Philosophers throughout the world have asked it. And for Christians, philosopher and layperson alike, the Bible is the standard of measure. It offers objective truth by which we judge right, wrong, good, and evil.

If the Bible has this much power, we should be asking the question, *Where did it come from?* We should also be asking, *Why should I trust it?* Even if you have never thought to ask those questions, many of your friends and loved ones are asking them!

Bibliology is the theology of the Bible. We're starting here because all theology begins with the revealed Word of God as recorded in these sixty-six books.

BIBLIOLOGY: *the theology of the Bible*

In the front of your Bible, any Bible, the table of contents organizes the books of the Bible into two major sections: Old Testament and New Testament. The word *testament* is another word for *covenant*. The first thirty-nine books are part of the *old covenant* between God and Israel. These texts are sacred in both Judaism and Christianity and are divided into three major sections:

- *Torah*: the first five books, also called Pentateuch (meaning "The Five")

- *Prophets*: the historical books (such as Judges and Kings) and prophetic literature (such as Isaiah and Ezekiel)
- *Writings*: poetic and proverbial books (such as Psalms and Ecclesiastes)

The New Testament, or *new covenant*, is made up of twenty-seven books of varied type:

- *Gospels*: the story of Jesus' life and ministry written by Matthew, Mark, Luke, and John
- *History of the early church*: the Acts of the apostles, which we often consider "part two" of Luke
- *Epistles*: letters such as First and Second Corinthians, Ephesians, First and Second Peter, and James
- *Apocalyptic literature*: Revelation

I must confess I often take the Bible for granted. It sits on my shelf or open in my lap, and I don't stop to wonder how it got there. Many of us never consider how these books got put together. After all, there are sixty-six books, written by more than a dozen different authors, over the course of three thousand years. How did they find one another? Did the Bible drop out of the sky, like an asteroid of thin pages and red-lettered words? It didn't—and that's great news because we couldn't trust it if it did!

The *historicity* of the Bible (its grounding in historical events, places, and people) gives credence to the story it tells.

That large wall ruler still hangs in our kitchen, now adjusted to the correct height. Last Sunday my daughter Adeline sat next to it, wearing tights and pigtails as she unwound string from her Sunday school craft. It was a telephone with two cups and a piece of string, surprisingly intact after being stretched across a church lobby between seven-year-old ears. She held it up eagerly, "Try it, Mom!" and goaded Josh and me into making a call. Stretched tight across the kitchen, whispering messages down the line, she strained to hear our words.

"I love you," I said.

"WHAT WAS THAT?" she yelled in reply. "I LUMP YOU?"

While our cup-and-string telephone conversations might be silly, some think the Bible was compiled by a similar method. God whispered vaguely into a prophet's ear, and the prophet made faulty attempts to record it: "What was that, God? 'Thou shalt not murmur'? Oh, *murder*! Got it."

But the Bible is not a cryptic gathering of vague spiritual ideas from random ancient men; nor is it a mystical book appearing, already compiled, into the hands of a single prophet. Terry Noble called it a two-part epic telling the redemptive plan of God.[1] W. A. Criswell said the story of salvation is a scarlet thread running from Genesis to Revelation.[2] Both scholars are saying the same thing: the Bible is one cohesive story told by many different people over many different centuries.

Can the Bible Be Trusted?

I was eighteen, almost out of high school, when one of my friends began exploring atheism. I had a small crush on him and wanted fodder for conversation, so I started reading some famous atheists— Dawkins, Hitchens, Harris, Nietchze.

I came away from those books with a sober realization: I needed to know why the Bible was worthy to be trusted. If I didn't, my Christianity had no leg to stand on. What I didn't have words for at the time was *the importance of bibliology*. My exposure to atheism revealed a scary truth, one that sunk in my heart like a stone: I didn't really *have* a bibliology. I just believed the Bible because it was the Word of God. I had failed to ask the question, *How* did it become the Word of God, and why do I believe that it is?

This Word we trust and turn to for spiritual guidance was compiled slowly over time. This surprises some of us—and even bothers us! Getting the Bible all at once would have been simpler. That's how we modern Christians received it. Many of us are given our first Bible at baptism or in Sunday school. Some people get theirs in prison or at church or at a secondhand store. One ministry leader I know was a Christian-curious ER doctor who stole a Bible from his own hospital waiting room! In all these situations, the reader is getting a complete, canonized, compiled Bible. This is a privilege, but it's not how the Bible has always existed.

Imagine the Bible as the epic story it is. It started thousands of years ago, in cultures different from ours, revealing the character of God in millennia. The story God revealed in these ancient cultures is still being told by the church today! While getting the Bible as one piece, magically from heaven, seems more straightforward, the Bible's progressive development makes it much more trustworthy. It reveals that God:

- shows Himself in history to real people, in real places, under real circumstances similar to ours today (albeit different historical context);
- has a plan for humanity and wishes to continue working with us and through us;
- uses restraint in how much of Himself He reveals at one time, out of mercy for our human understanding;
- respects cultural context; and
- is doing something far greater than we can imagine.

In contrast, there are some cults and religions whose sacred books are given all at once to a single prophet. Such revelation lacks more than one witness (a fundamental biblical value), accountability to community, and a standard of measure. In contrast, the Bible's books were given to multiple prophets, apostles, and disciples. They were written in different eras but contain content that consistently upholds who God is and what He is doing in the world. God's character is the ultimate measure of "canon."

CANON: *a collection of books able to tell us who God is and how we should live in relationship to Him*

Picture my ruler again, hanging on the kitchen wall. Before the ruler was the *kanon. Kanon* is the Greek word for "reed" (yes, the kind in which baby Moses was found). Coincidentally, the reed referenced by this Greek word grows in Egypt. In the ancient world, these reeds were cut, dried, and used as a standard of measure. Over time the term *kanon* came to represent a general standard of measure and morphed into the word *canon*, which we use today to mean "a rule . . . by which something is judged" and "an authoritative list of books accepted as Holy Scripture."[3]

How Did the Bible Come to Be?

The books in our Bible today are there because the early church and its leadership judged them as (1) historically trustworthy, (2) doctrinally consistent, and (3) connected to eyewitnesses. The process of choosing what books can be treated as Scripture is called *canonization*.

The first five books of the Bible are called the Torah, or Pentateuch. Tradition says Moses wrote these books with some editing by Joshua after Moses died. It is more likely that Moses wrote portions, and the rest was edited and compiled closer to the fifth or sixth century BC. It is likely that someone may have done edits because Moses' death is recorded in the text, and also because of brief insertions such as, "Moses was a very humble man, more humble than anyone else on the face of the earth" (Numbers 12:3).[4] (Kudos to Moses if he penned with such self-confidence, but scholars believe Joshua or a scribe added this later.) The Torah is the centerpiece of Jewish theology, and it is the Torah Jesus based His teaching on. Almost all the debates Jesus had with the religious leaders had to do with Torah law.

The Torah was quickly canonized by the Israelites, deemed authoritative for spiritual guidance and civil law. These books are ancient, and we often need help to understand them, but understanding them is vital to the rest of the story!

The next group of books to be added to the Bible—still before Christ—were the prophetic books and the "writings," such as Psalms, Proverbs, Ecclesiastes, and Song of Songs. These books are the outworking of Moses' law. We see songs about God's character, wisdom for following God's law, and prophecies about what will happen if God's people depart from His ways.[5]

The complete Old Testament, made up of thirty-nine historical, legal, prophetic, and poetic texts, was quickly received by the Jewish people and the non-Jewish people residing with them. The Old Testament was a guide for the spiritual life of believers before Jesus came to earth. The *Holman Illustrated Bible Dictionary* says this directly: "As each book of the Old Testament was written, its authority as the revealed Word of God evoked the immediate embracing of it as sacred and binding."[6]

Between the Old and New Testaments was a four-hundred-year span of time that scholars often call "the silent period." During these years the Jews were persecuted and the Maccabean rebellion took place (this is celebrated today through the festival of Hanukkah). This silent period ended with the birth of Jesus, the fulfillment of Old Testament prophecy. Two of the four Gospels, Matthew and Luke, record this momentous event. While all four Gospels record Jesus' life and ministry, each shares a different perspective on what He did and said.

Before the first century concluded, congregations were referring to these eyewitness texts as authoritative. Even earlier, Peter referred to Paul's letters as Scripture (2 Peter 3:15–16) and Paul cited Luke's gospel as Scripture (1 Timothy 5:18). The Gospels and the letters of our New Testament were circulated to groups of Christians around the Middle East and Asia for encouragement and instruction. By the third and fourth centuries AD, lists of canonical books could be found confirming a Bible almost identical to ours today.

Knowing how quickly the Bible was received, revered, and rooted in historical truth helps us understand why Christians seek it for guidance on life and behavior. We aren't the first people to do this; we have an ancestry of faith in the Word of God! The Bible was written for all people in all times. However, knowing how it was compiled is only the first step in appreciating its authority. The next step involves the nature of the writing itself: the Bible as literature.

What Are the Literary Genres in the Bible?

Before studying religion at a liberal arts university, I attended community college in my hometown. Community college night classes come in all shapes and sizes—I took many, each one its own grab bag of opinions and characters. An English class I took fell during a presidential election and our group was eager to discuss it, perhaps more than the stories we were supposed to read. The class tables were set around the room in a giant square as if we were about to do a script reading for an upcoming television series. There was no hiding from our professor, who stood in the middle, as we read aloud

GENRE: *a type of literary composition*

strange, slightly off-color stories from a *Norton's Anthology* that weighed twenty pounds.

I learned two things in that class: when to keep my opinion to myself, and that when it comes to literature, *genre matters.*

As foreign as it may seem to classify it this way, the Bible is literature. Secular scholars study it as such, but the Christian reverence for Scripture can make us forgetful of what it is we're reading. Identifying genre is helpful when drawing out interpretation. If we want to interpret the Bible rightly and understand its authority, we have to take note of the genre we're reading.

If I handed you a book and told you it was a mystery, you'd be pretty annoyed on page seventy-five when you discovered, after much wasted time, that I'd *actually* handed you a sappy romance. Your expectation was set! You were looking for the plot, the case, the conflict. The *genre* of the book had already told your brain what to look for in the text. We can use this to our advantage when studying the Bible.

Genre guides our understanding of not only the author's intent but also how the text's message impacts our lives today. A healthy bibliology begins with healthy literacy. Being able to see the full range of meaning intended by the biblical writers helps us accurately apply the Bible to life.

Here are some ways to identify genre and read it well:

- **HISTORY:** Historical narrative—like Joshua, Judges, Kings, First and Second Chronicles, Samuel, and Acts—is written to tell a story. It is full of places and people important to the story. These records weren't meant to be immediately moralized like *Aesop's Fables*; they were intended to record the history of

God's interactions with people on earth. We best discern the theological principles in these passages when we don't look for immediate application but instead note the setting, context, people, and actions of God.

- **LAW:** Books like Leviticus, Numbers, and Deuteronomy contain a mixture of legal code and historical narrative. These are the books we tend to struggle with the most. They seem dry, boring, and irrelevant to us—but they aren't! The books of law show us how much God wanted humans to be able to live with Him. He wanted it so much, He created a law to make communion with Himself possible. God chose to use a specific nation and moral code to set apart a people in the world as a "city on a hill," a template for what the church would be thousands of years later.

- In these books, take note of the moral themes and expectations that appear most often: love God, honor others, and so on. Scholars divide biblical law into three types: civil, ceremonial, and moral. Civil laws have to do with the governance of Israel as a nation ruled by God. Ceremonial laws relate to temple or tabernacle worship. Moral laws are summed up in the Ten Commandments and expressed in more detail through Leviticus and Deuteronomy. While we no longer observe the civil laws because we do not live in ancient Israel, and the ceremonial laws apply to Jewish Christians but not to Gentiles, the moral laws are reaffirmed in the New Testament and apply to all of us today.

- **PROPHECY:** The prophetic books are usually divided into two sections: the major prophets (Ezekiel, Jeremiah, Isaiah) and the minor prophets (Amos, Obadiah, Hosea, etc.). Major and minor don't indicate more or less importance, rather the size of the books themselves. Major prophetic books are significantly longer than minor prophetic books. These prophetic books should be read alongside the historical narrative of

First and Second Kings and First and Second Chronicles, since much of what happens in them coincides with the events recorded there. Prophetic books are often repetitive because the prophets were trying to make a point and warn their society about the consequences of sin. Some prophetic books sound quite harsh until you understand what Israel was doing: idol worship, child sacrifice, sexual promiscuity, and other pagan cultural practices.

- **GOSPEL:** The Gospels are divided into the Synoptics (Matthew, Mark, and Luke) and John. The Synoptics were written as testimonies of Jesus' life and ministry, and they're called Synoptics because they're similar to one another in narrative. John, however, was written specifically for evangelism and to give further proof of Jesus' divinity. All four of the Gospels quote extensively from the Old Testament, both in Jesus' direct quotes and as proof of how Jesus fulfilled Old Testament prophecy.

- **EPISTLE:** Epistles are letters, often written to specific churches and circulated throughout a city or province for the edification of the Christian population there. The epistles in the Bible are named either after the author (for example, James, Peter) or after the recipient (for example, Colossians, Philippians, Corinthians). Because the letters were written to specific people, it is helpful in our understanding to look up information about those groups before reading the letter sent to them. The principles shared in the letters are universal, but their specific context helps us understand the author's intent.

- **APOCALYPTIC:** Apocalyptic literature is a little wild. We see it in Revelation and also in parts of Daniel. These books utilize a wide range of imagery to depict a spiritual point. Poetry, prophecy, and allegory all play a part. Much of what we see in this type of literature is not meant to be taken at face value; for instance, we should not assume that the locusts with tails like horses in Revelation 9 will actually be locusts with hairy tails! Rather, it's likely an image to represent the evil of the creature. Read apocalyptic literature looking for the big picture and noting any part that is connected to another book of the Bible.

Who Told the Authors to Write the Bible?

This brings us to the question of the biblical writers themselves. How did they know to write all of this down? Certainly, some books recount that God told them to write the book (like Isaiah and Revelation). But many others don't indicate such instructions. Who told the authors what to write, and why do we think it was God?

To answer these questions we use three *i* words associated with bibliology. These words also give us theological glasses through which to view the Bible. The nature of these three words has been debated by scholars over the course of church history. Most conservative scholars (those who stay close to the original text and traditional interpretation) adhere to these words in some way. They are *inspiration, inerrancy,* and *infallibility.*

Inspiration

Sometimes I coach writers, and when I do, I teach them not to rely on "inspiration" for when and how to write. Many writers use the word *inspiration* to mean a feeling or urge to write or a bright idea. Writers who depend on feeling have a hard time being consistent in the long run. Inspiration of that kind is fleeting.

However, when we talk about the Bible being "inspired," we're not referring to a passing emotion or a prophet's bright idea. The biblical writers didn't wake up one day after some bad pizza and think, *You know, I think I heard God last night. I'm gonna write a book about it.* (Interesting as such a book might have been!) Neither is *inspiration* New Age "automatic writing," where a prophet taps into God's Spirit and writes whatever comes to him in a trance. Yes, prophets had visions and recorded them, but they were not required to empty their minds or hold a seance with a spirit to do so.

Scriptural *inspiration* means the Bible was initiated by God, breathed out by His Spirit through human agents in a specific historical context. That's powerful! It means that the things recorded about God's interactions with humanity have authority and weight. The inspiration and initiation of God is visible in almost every book of the Bible. In the English Standard Version, the phrase "thus says the Lord" occurs 417 times. "The Lord said" occurs 275 times.[7] God's initiation and interaction with His Word are evidenced in the text.

And yet inspiration is a little more complicated than this.

Scholars define two types of inspiration: *verbal* and *plenary.*

- Verbal inspiration means that every single word of the Bible (not just its concepts) was directly inspired by God Himself and was communicated from God to people.
- Plenary inspiration means that the whole Bible (from lengthy genealogies to John 3:16) carries God's authority. Jesus affirmed this truth in Luke 16:17 when He said, "It is easier for heaven and earth to pass away than for one stroke of a letter in the law to drop out" (HCSB).

Together this creates a micro-macro inspiration. The Bible came from God, period. But why? Or how?

In 2 Timothy 3:16–17, Paul said, "All Scripture is breathed out by God and profitable for teaching, for reproof, for correction, and for training in righteousness, that the man of God may be complete, equipped for every good work" (ESV). This tells us the essential nature of Scripture for spiritual maturity and growth. We cannot be competent and equipped for every good work apart from the Word of God. If we want to be mature Christians, then we need to be in the Word.

But why would the Word of God change us? Paul said it is because it's breathed out by God. The phrase "breathed out" has to do with the Holy Spirit because the word for Holy Spirit means "breath." The very Spirit of God inspired these words and made them profitable for teaching, reproof, correction, and training in righteousness—in other words, for growing people up in what is good.

As if this weren't enough, Peter said something similar in 2 Peter 1:21: "No prophecy was ever produced by the will of man, but men spoke from God as they were carried along by the Holy Spirit" (ESV). Here's another founding father of our faith, Peter, writing the exact same thing as Paul, declaring that all of Scripture is inspired by God, led by the Holy Spirit, and only *written* by men. They didn't do this by their own will; it was because of God's inspiration. God was working through the instrument of human personality, and though God worked through historical context and even the authors' writing styles, the inspiration to write came from the Lord.

The biblical authors stated outright that the words they shared were from God (for example, Exodus 17:14; Jeremiah 1:9; Ezekiel 1:3; Hosea 1:1). Jesus did too! He affirmed the authority of the Old Testament (the Bible of His day) by quoting it liberally in response to spiritual questions, including those that questioned His deity and authority (Matthew 19:4–5; Mark 12:36).

Inerrancy

Inerrancy is a word used to say that the Bible is not in error. This means Scripture makes good on its claims; it achieves what the authors were aiming for. This doesn't mean there's never a copyediting error or a discrepancy between two documents (the Bible was hand-copied until the invention of the printing press), but none of those discrepancies changed the big-picture story, the gospel message, or the doctrine. They were simply copy errors or slight differences in the documents that did not impact the theological reading.

As one scholar has noted,

> The only error-free documents were the originals. While no one has ever denied that mistakes can be found in the various copies that have been made, this fact has nothing to do with the original. Furthermore, the closer we get to the original wording of the text, we find that the errors become less and less. . . . The variant readings that do exist do not threaten any doctrine of Scripture, or any command that God gives to believers. . . . The sense of any passage can be gathered from the immediate context—the variants in the manuscripts do not affect the overall content.[8]

The Bible we have today was handed down with incredible accuracy, especially given the times in which it was translated and transmitted. When the Dead Sea Scrolls were discovered in 1947, they proved that the Old Testament had been copied consistently, with almost zero changes, for thousands of years. A scroll of Isaiah from among the Dead Sea Scrolls (dated about 100 BC) agreed almost to the letter with the Masoretic texts from a thousand years later.

Infallibility

Inerrancy and *infallibility* might sound like trendy baby names for twin girls, but as we've seen, the meaning is a little deeper than that. *Inerrancy* means without error; *infallibility* means unable to deceive. When we use the word *infallible* for the Bible, we are saying that nothing in the text is able to deceive us or lead us away from God Himself. Certainly, *teachers* may misinterpret these texts and lead people astray, but the Word accurately taught and understood will never do so.

This is why the New Testament writers were so vehement against false teaching (2 Timothy 4; Acts 20; 2 Peter 3; 1 John 4). It's also why we need to check others' teaching *against* Scripture, like the Bereans were commended for in Acts 17:11, when they compared Paul's and Silas's teaching to the Old Testament to "see if these things were so" (ESV). When we rightly understand the Bible, it will never deceive us or lead us away from the path of life. These words will always direct us *toward* it.

We can think of the three *i*'s of the Bible as *eyes*. They give us a view of truth. The lenses of inspiration, inerrancy, and infallibility lead us to the conclusion scholars have held for thousands of years: We can trust the Bible's historical accuracy and spiritual authority. And because this is true, we can allow it to lead our lives. This doesn't mean we interpret every passage at face value, since the authors sometimes used symbolism to express concepts about God. But it does require respect for the Bible's authority and its ability to guide our life decisions.

Does the Bible Really Get to Tell Me How to Live?

Let's revisit the children's height ruler hanging on my farmhouse wall. Since the things it measured weren't essential to life, it did no harm to measure incorrectly. Adeline thought she was a foot taller than she was for a few months, but no one was set on a path of destruction because of it!

However, without an objective, authoritative source of truth—a *kanon* by which to measure what is right and wrong—much harm *is* accomplished. The "ruler" becomes whatever we feel is most important: our emotions, our sexual desires, our political ideals. The things that should be *informed by* objective truth instead become the measure of truth itself. The result is a multiplicity of "kanons" that differ wildly from person to person.

We see this happen in the mantras "find your truth" and "live your truth." Our culture considers truth to be subjective. Truth is whatever you want it to be.

We know such an idea could not survive scientific testing. Certain things must be or not be; they can't be redefined from person to person. But what about morality? Can morality be subjective? The Bible says no. On issues of life, sex, spirituality, and relationships, the Bible speaks boldly for an ethic of honor and love. And because Scripture is historical, spiritual, and able to guide into all life, we can trust its authority.

As theologian John Stott said, "We must allow the Word of God to confront us, to disturb our security, to undermine our complacency and to overthrow our patterns of thought and behavior."[9] Or to put it in the plainer language of writer Andrena Sawyer, "We can't weaponize Scripture when it defends our behavior and reject it when it convicts us."[10]

Scripture is not just meant for other people. It is not to be used just for pointing out sin in others; it is for the refining of our own character. The authority of the Bible changes *us* before it changes the world. If we follow Jesus, we must allow the words Jesus inspired to change, convict, and transform us. The Bible's impact on *us* has priority over the Bible's impact on others.

This does not mean everyone will affirm the Bible's truth. Some people will reject the biblical narrative and fall into unbelief. This unbelief can take three forms: emotional, rational, and volitional. Emotional unbelief has to do with our experiences: "I was hurt by the church, so I don't trust the Bible." Rational unbelief has to do with evidence: "I don't see enough historical evidence to trust the Bible." Volitional unbelief is a willful rejection of the Bible, when someone remains unconvinced by experience or evidence.

The emotional and rational responses can sometimes be worked through with gentle discussions and quality resources. Occasionally, we can reach people who've been hurt by the church or are questioning the Bible with a kind and truthful explanation. But those who give in to volitional unbelief are like the people described in Ephesians 4:18: "They are darkened in their understanding, alienated from the life of God because of the ignorance that is in them, due to their hardness of heart" (ESV). Hardness of heart cannot be broken with more facts or testimonies. Only the Lord Himself, who longs for all people to know Him through His Word, can reach the ones set on rejecting Him.

Isn't that the whole point of Scripture? It's a story of the initiating, loving, redeeming God who chases down the imperfect and rebellious, even when He knows they'll reject His truth. He does not wish for any to perish (2 Peter 3:9). The Word of God is the gospel of Christ, which is "the power of God that brings salvation to everyone who believes" (Romans 1:16). The authoritative beauty of the Bible will not return void.

As the Lord says in Isaiah 55:11, "So is my word that goes out from my mouth: It will not return to me empty, but will accomplish what I desire and achieve the purpose for which I sent it." The Bible has authority and power because God has authority and power.

Though written in a distant time, the Bible's truths are relevant for us today. God was willing to enter into the raw human experience in an ancient culture to reveal His love. He was willing to record Himself within the arc of human darkness and shame, to reveal that He is not afraid of sin or Satan but has come to redeem and restore regardless of culture or age. The Bible is the timeless story of God's reaching, holding, never-giving-up love, and it's a story we get to participate in. The more we celebrate and embrace the Word of God, the better we know the God who breathed it. The Bible is the foundation of our theology, our worship, and our experience of Christ. It's hard to let something that valuable gather dust on the shelf!

If we want to become theologians, we have to start where theologians begin: the Word of God. Through this breathed-out Word our own lungs are filled with air, empowering us to live the Christian life God desires. The Word is life, lamp, and light (Psalm 119:105). The Bible is the foundation of our Christianity, and the reason C. S. Lewis could say in his book *The Weight of Glory*, "I believe in Christianity as I believe that the Sun has risen, not only because I see it, but because by it I see everything else."[11]

By what light do we see the world? By what ruler, what *kanon*, do we measure truth? For us, there is one answer: the Word of God.

CHAPTERS AND VERSE DIVISIONS

The Bible did not come to us initially as a single compiled document or with the structure of chapters and verses. The original texts were written on scrolls—the Old Testament in Hebrew, the New Testament in Greek. In the 1200s, Archbishop of Canterbury Stephen Langton added chapter numbers to the Vulgate, the Latin translation of the Bible. Three centuries later in the 1550s, a monk named Robertus Stephanus added verses to his Greek New Testament. We still use this model of chapters and verses today.

MARCION

DID YOU KNOW? The early church spent a lot of time hammering out the essential doctrines of Christianity. One of those doctrines had to do with bibliology: What books do we trust to shape our view of God? This topic became urgent to the church when a wealthy shipowner's son, Marcion, became a pastor and created his own "canon."

Marcion was raised on Scripture, both Old and New Testament. But he didn't like the Old Testament God; he believed the Old Testament presented a "lesser deity" than Jesus. After editing, Marcion's canon consisted of the gospel of Luke and ten of Paul's letters. This biblical hack job put the church into overdrive. Marcion was excommunicated (removed from church fellowship), but rather than repent, he took his edited Bible and evangelized for a "Christ" disconnected from history and Scripture.

Sadly, Marcion is not an isolated example. The same pattern emerges today: The Bible is edited to fit what teachers find suited to their own worldviews and fleshly desires. Like the church in the second century, we need to know why both the Old and New Testaments are essential to Christianity and how to answer the questions of skeptics.

Chapter 2

Theology: A Loving and Holy Father

THE DOCTRINE OF GOD

I came to Christ because of pornography.

At twelve I was exposed to an erotica novel at a garage sale. Erotica novels are romance novels with sexually explicit scenes; they're essentially pornography in book form. The book had no cover and, thinking it might be a Boxcar Children or Nancy Drew, I picked it up. I was intrigued, then ashamed, and I threw the book away from me. But I was also curious.

The shame drove my curiosity into secrecy, and as I continued consuming the novels, I harbored my struggle for years. Over the next three years, I found myself confused, angry, and helpless in my sin and shame. I didn't know where to turn, I was too embarrassed to tell my parents, and I didn't want anyone in my friend group to know my situation. While I wouldn't choose to relive that lonely season, it drove me to the one Person I knew I could trust: Christ.

Desperate for an answer, I began to pray. I began to ask questions: *Does God really love me? What does it mean that Jesus died for my sins? How could God tolerate me when I keep exposing myself to this trash?* Up to that point I had been hardened to the things of God. I had no interest in worship at church, I was bored by sermons, and I didn't have any desire to honor my parents or love my siblings. I was a challenging child and a little bit proud of it. But this new realization of my helplessness drove me to seek an answer.

I came to Christ in the back ten acres of our family farm, alone at sunset, writing in a journal bedecked with sunflowers. Jesus met me there, and my heart changed. But my life didn't—at least not right away.

My struggle with erotica would be an ongoing battle for the next decade. But underneath that struggle was something deeper, the real reason for my sexual stronghold. It actually had less to do with sex and a lot to do with my view of God. I viewed God as a judge: righteous, just, too holy for sin, offering Christ to save me but doing so with some reluctance. I believed God *loved* me (John 3:16!) but I did not believe God *liked* me. He tolerated me. He was a distant and difficult Father, unlike even my earthly father—a good man—and I preferred to keep my distance from Him. I battled my sin, never feeling as though I was forgiven, never truly gaining victory, and never feeling at rest in the affection of God.

If you're like most Christians, you probably resonate with some part of my story. Perhaps not the pornography portion, but maybe the shame portion. Or the reluctance to accept God's love. Or the disbelief in His kindness. But it's important to know that our theology of God the Father affects how we interact with all the other "ologies" of Christianity. After all, if God isn't kind, if He is an intolerant and reluctant Father, then we are never truly safe in our attachment to Him.

The Bible upends these assumptions. The God of the Old Testament is the same as Jesus in the New, and the closer we study it, the more apparent this becomes. As we explore the character of God, we find Him far kinder, greater, and gentler than we ever imagined.

Let God Define Himself

To truly embrace God's character, we have to destroy the assumptions we make about who He is—and we all have assumptions. It's amazing how we project our own experiences or unanswered prayers back onto God. While some of this is to be expected (we're human!), we must be honest enough to check these assumptions against what Scripture, in its context, says about God.

We read Old Testament passages through the Western bias of a culture enamored with love and unacquainted with true justice. Ancient Middle Eastern culture was built not on feelings of love but on structures of honor and shame; family honor, respect for elders, and integrity held the utmost importance. Our cultural differences cause us to struggle to form an accurate picture of the God of Israel. We have no framework for Him.

Fortunately for us, the Bible gives us a framework if we take the time to understand it!

The God of the Old Testament is often accused of being vindictive, wrathful, violent, and unloving. In contrast, many people point to Jesus as loving, kind, nonviolent, and accepting. The two are presented as oppositional forces, when in fact they are two sides of the same coin. Jesus is and was God. God sent and is one with Jesus. The Holy Spirit is the very essence of Christ given for our growth. We'll talk more about the Trinity specifically in a moment, but it's important not to splice apart these Persons of God based on our own feelings about love and wrath.

Instead, we should be considering the following questions:

- Why did God command firm judgments for sin in the Old Testament law?
- Why did God send Jesus?
- What did Jesus say about God?

We must deal in the revealed Word of God, not just our feelings about that Word. When we take the time to wrestle with these texts and let them teach us about who the Father is, we come away far more secure in His love for us.

There is so much that could be said—and has been said—about God. The theology of God the Father fills entire books and systematic theologies. Here we're going to focus on some of the most evident truths found in Scripture and the fundamentals of Christian doctrine. We'll see these principles emerge in other "ologies" later as well! Let's start with one of the more complicated but most fought-for doctrines of the church: the Trinity.

God Is Trinity

Every Saint Patrick's Day parents attempt to teach the Trinity with strained analogies to three-leafed clovers. When it's not St. Paddy's, we use analogies to water, describing it as one substance, able to present itself in three ways: liquid, solid, or gas. But any analogy we use to describe the Trinity will fall short. The Trinity is a truly *mystical*, spiritual doctrine; it's hard to explain and sometimes hard to understand. And yet our early church fathers considered it so important that they fought for it in books, letters, and councils over hundreds of years.

Many people struggle with the idea of Trinity. Some struggle to understand how three *Persons* of God isn't the same as *three gods*. The unique personhood of Father, Son, and Spirit simply means they are distinct. The Father is not the Son, the Son is not the Spirit, the

Spirit is not the Father, and so on. In the Bible, the Father sent Jesus into the world and Jesus left the Spirit with the church. For this to occur, they cannot be the same Person. Some scholars summarize this difference by saying each member of the Trinity has a distinct center of consciousness. This is how Christianity can be a monotheistic religion (a religion with one god), and yet we talk about God, Jesus, and the Holy Spirit as individual entities or Persons. If your mind spins a little, that's understandable; this is one of the most essential yet complicated doctrines of our faith.

In his book *Delighting in the Trinity*, theologian Michael Reeves outlines the importance of God's triune nature, saying, "I could believe in the death of a man called Jesus, I could believe in his bodily resurrection, I could even believe in a salvation by grace alone; but if I do not believe in this God, then, quite simply, I am not a Christian. And so, because the Christian God is triune, the Trinity is the governing center of all Christian belief."[1]

This is a bold statement. But it gets to be bold because it's true. If God is triune (three in One), then everything we know about Him and every truth we hold points back to this three-in-one nature. We can't rightly understand Jesus' life, death, or ministry apart from the Father who sent Him or the Spirit He left behind. We can't understand Christian life today, led by the Spirit, without Jesus' atoning sacrifice, and we can't understand the point of any of it without the God revealed in the Old Testament books. In a sense, the Trinity traps us into the truth. Without the Trinity, there is no Christianity, and there is no Christianity if God is not triune.

Inevitably this leaves us with questions. If God is not three separate gods, nor a cosmic "shape-shifter" moving between godlike personalities, how do we understand Him? The simplest way to describe the doctrine of Trinity is that God is one, existing in three Persons; He is equal, eternal, and distinct, yet unified in Himself. At the risk of falling short with yet another analogy, one might describe the Godhead like a human being who is at the same time daughter, sister, and mother. None of these roles make her any less human in essence. She is three, yet she is one. However, this analogy falls flat as well since those three "roles" aren't distinct Persons like the Father, Spirit, and Son, but it might give us a slightly clearer picture of what Scripture describes. Father John Behr says the Father, Son, and Spirit "are the same or one in essence" yet distinct and personal.[2]

The Trinity can be a divisive doctrine. It is the doctrine that sets us apart from Islam, Jehovah's Witnesses, and the Church of Jesus Christ of Latter-day Saints (Mormons). Each of these affirm God and Jesus in some capacity, but all of them deny the Trinity. The trinitarian doctrine drove the church to develop the Apostles' Creed and later on the Nicene Creed, which set in stone a set of beliefs the apostles taught and the early church affirmed.

Before we move on to some other truths about God the Father, we must ask, What's the real-life impact of the Trinity? It actually has a lot to do with God's love. In other monotheistic religions, the main "man upstairs" is a solitary being. He is, as Michael Reeves says, "an inevitably self-centered being."[3]

Completely solitary gods create people out of a desire for servants or slaves or sexual partners, not out of a desire to truly love. But the Christian God is different. This God is One, but He is expressed in Three, and these Three all have fellowship in the One. They are a *community* of holy love. And from this community of holy love pours out *love in community*. God created humanity. He didn't create a single human but two, and from those two He fully expected a fruitful and multiplied world. Why? So He could dwell with them and be their God (Exodus 29:45).

The community of the Trinity created the community of humanity, which was intended to commune in unity: God and human, forever. Sin ruined this intention, but in the final restoration God's original goal will be achieved. The triune God is a communal God, a loving God, and He can be no other kind.

God Is Love

God is love because God is Trinity. This leads us to explore God's love, which is perhaps His most monopolized and misinterpreted attribute. What does it mean that God *is* love (1 John 4:8)? Here's how John described it:

> Beloved, let us love one another, for love is from God, and whoever loves has been born of God and knows God. Anyone who does not love does not know God, because God is love. In this the love of God was made manifest among us, that God sent his only Son into the world, so that we might live through him. In this is love, not that we have loved God but that he loved us and sent his Son to be the propitiation for our sins. Beloved, if God so loved us, we also ought to love one another. (1 John 4:7–11 ESV)

John's passage teaches us three things about God's love: love is God's essence (v. 8), God's love is sacrificial and self-giving (vv. 9–10), and God's love is transforming—those who experience it want to give love to others (v. 11).

This definition of love diverges from our culture's ideals. To love someone today can mean a range of things, including but not limited to endorsement, affirmation, unquestioning support, and attention. If you don't affirm the choices someone makes—no matter how damaging or unwise—you're deemed "unloving." But how does this align with love as God defines it?

The love of Christ is self-giving and sacrificial. It's also wise. God's love is not in opposition to attributes like holiness and righteousness; it is *complementary* to them. In other words, these are not two poles on a globe but two sides of the same coin. You can't have love without justice and truth, and you can't have true justice without love.

When we as a modern culture moved ourselves away from God,

we separated ourselves from both justice and love. Our justice is polluted by selfish opinions and lack of consideration for others; our love is diluted by the mistaken idea that affection equals endorsement. The Christian God upends these assumptions. His love will not be manipulated or separated from truth, and yet it is this truthful, faithful, *hesed* love (a "completely undeserved kindness and generosity"[4]) that chases us down and seeks us in our sin: "In Jesus, God has taken the initiative to seek out the sinner, to bring the lost into the blessing of his reign. He was, in short, the seeking God."[5]

Jesus proved that God's heart, holy as it is, is not to separate from the sinner but to invite the sinner to experience the Father's love. Of course, humans may choose to reject that love, and by doing so they embrace separation. That choice has always been an option. But Jesus revealed God's seeking, loving heart to humanity by entering into a relationship with people who needed the transformative love of God. This exposure to the Father's heart changed them—and it changes us.

It changed me.

In the midst of my addiction to erotic fiction, I rode a pendulum between repentance and fear. I repented of my sin because I knew it was wrong. I was objectifying the people in these stories, objectifying myself, and objectifying my sexuality. I was filling my mind with the opposite of what is pure, noble, and praiseworthy (Philippians 4:8). But my motivation for repentance wasn't the love of God, at least not in those early years. My motivation was fear. I repented because I was afraid of God, afraid of sin, and afraid of what might happen if I lived there. In a way I think that was a healthy fear. Yes, we should recognize the consequences of sin and take them seriously. However, in Scripture such fear is always tempered by the open arms of God. But I didn't see His arms as open; I saw them as crossed.

I believed this judging God saw my sin, and I felt shamefully exposed. At seventeen, a few years after I came to Christ and five years into the addiction, I read a book about God's love. The sun rose, a switch flipped, and I understood why I continued to repeat the same patterns over and over. *I did not trust God's love.* My repentance was genuine, but because I never felt truly attached to God, secure in His love for me and His grace over my sin, I returned to what felt safe: my sin. Of course, it wasn't safe—it was damaging—but the familiarity deceived me. I was so unfamiliar with the affection of God that I ran to the very thing destroying my heart.

The love of God is the glue of Scripture. It's the binding of the theological truths we study. The Christian God is distinct because He is, in every part of His being, love. Love is *Him.* There is no love in this world that can exist apart from Him. Every human love is an echo of the original *hesed*, the faithful, seeking love, brave enough to redeem the darkest sinner you know—even if that sinner is you.

"We have come to know and to believe the love that God has for us. God is love, and whoever abides in love abides in God, and God abides in him" (1 John 4:16 ESV).

We know God's love. But do we believe it? Until we do, we can't live in it. Abiding comes from believing. God's love is real, and it is *for you*. "For God so loved the world [you] that he gave his one and only Son, that whoever [you] believes in him shall not perish but have eternal life" (John 3:16, brackets added). Eternal life is not just beyond death. It's real life *now*. It's real life free from addiction and dependency and anger and bitterness. It's real life knowing and believing God's love is *for you*, not just for everyone else.

God Is Holy

The Hebrew word for *holy* means "separate" or "set apart."[6] God is utterly unlike us; He is perfect, sinless, and completely good. His holiness is the guarantor of His love! Because God is so perfectly holy, we can trust that His love is unstained by self-interest. This is one reason God's love and holiness can't be pitted against each other but must instead be viewed as one complementary unit, a symbiotic relationship of love and purity.

God's holiness is a major theme in the Bible. God affirmed His holiness to Israel. Jesus affirmed God's holiness in His ministry. The apostles affirmed God's holiness to the church.

- "Who is like you, O LORD, among the gods? Who is like you, majestic in holiness, awesome in glorious deeds, doing wonders?" (Exodus 15:11 ESV).
- "Thus says the One who is high and lifted up, who inhabits eternity, whose name is Holy: 'I dwell in the high and holy place, and also with him who is of a contrite and lowly spirit, to revive the spirit of the lowly, and to revive the heart of the contrite'" (Isaiah 57:15 ESV).
- "God has not called us for impurity, but in holiness" (1 Thessalonians 4:7 ESV).
- "It is written, 'You shall be holy, for I am holy'" (1 Peter 1:16 ESV).

Because God is holy, we, His children, are expected to be holy. All moral behavior is rooted in the character of a holy and righteous God. When we think about God's moral law—expressed in the Ten Commandments (Exodus 20) and again in the fruit of the Spirit (Galatians 5)—we don't treat these things as inconveniences. We see them as just and loving. No one wants to endorse murder, envy, and robbery, at least no one with an awakened conscience. And yet when we judge God as "angry" or "wrathful" for His holiness, we're undermining the foundation for all moral behavior. God should be wrathful against murder. He should be angry when people envy and steal and wound other image bearers. God is wrathful against sin because God is *love*, and that love is perfectly holy in all its ways.

This is how theologian R.C. Sproul described sin against the love of God:

> Sin is cosmic treason. Sin is treason against a perfectly pure Sovereign. It is an act of supreme ingratitude toward the One to whom we owe everything, to the One who has given us life itself. Have you ever considered the deeper implications of the slightest sin, of the most minute peccadillo? What are we saying to our Creator when we disobey Him at the slightest point? We are saying no to the righteousness of God. We are saying, "God, Your law is not good. My judgment is better than Yours. Your authority does not apply to me. I am above and beyond Your jurisdiction. I have the right to do what I want to do, not what You command me to do."[7]

The human understanding of holiness is tainted by our own tendency toward self-interest. Unless we are daily exposed to the true nature of God, we are prone to make allowances for our own pet sins. We may try to downplay God's holiness, failing to recognize how doing so undermines every objective statement we make. We can make no moral judgments if there is no moral Judge. God's holiness is fundamental—not just for Christianity but for all worldviews—for without an objective moral standard, we can make no truth statements about right or wrong. Every time we create a law or seek justice or call something "good," we're trapped into the necessity of a moral judge. God's holiness is that judge. It is vital that Christians understand both God's holiness and His love. Many believers tend to emphasize one over the other, leading to an imbalanced and extreme theology. If God is only holy and not loving, there is no hope for us, no safety in His affection. If God is all love and no holiness, my behavior doesn't matter and I am left in my sins, hurting other image bearers with my selfish deeds. God's love calls us to holiness *so that* we love others effectively and, in doing so, bless the world.

God Is Just

"The Rock, his work is perfect, for all his ways are justice. A God of faithfulness and without iniquity, just and upright is he" (Deuteronomy 32:4 ESV).

My understanding of God's love and holiness together led me to believe God's *justice*. This justice freed me from my addiction to pornography and erotica because I knew God was right in His sexual ethic. He was right to want honor for my body and the bodies of others. He was right to call my desires into alignment with His. He was right to create boundaries for my sexual desires within either celibacy or covenant marriage and to call me up to a satisfaction outside of romantic idolatry.

Understanding God's justice requires a foundation in both love and holiness. Without love, God's justice is ruthless. Without holiness, God's justice is untrue.

The spirit of the modern age is social justice. But this phrase alone can mean a dozen things! Some Christians cringe and side-eye those two words; others wear them proudly. And yet we can agree that Christians should care immensely about justice because *God is just*. That justice, however, must be biblically defined. It must also be socially active or it's a justice of lip service alone.

In a series on biblical justice, pastor and theologian Tim Keller says this of God's just nature:

> God's justice is both retributive and reparative. It not only punishes evildoing, but it restores those who are victims of injustice. . . . As the Judge of all the earth, the Lord will finally give everyone what justice dictates is due to them (Acts 17:30–31). But he will also restore and "renew all things" so there is no more evil, suffering, or death (Matthew 19:28). Both his retributive and remunerative justice will come to final fulfillment at the end of history, and we will live in a new heavens and new earth filled

with *dikaiosune*—justice (2 Peter 3:13). These basic themes work themselves out in four facets of biblical justice. Biblical justice is characterized by: radical generosity, universal equality, life-changing advocacy, and asymmetrical responsibility.[8]

God's just nature and desire to protect those who are being unjustly treated should motivate Christians to desire the same. Though Christians may disagree on *how* such justice should be accomplished, there should be no debate that justice is not just an eternal reality but also a present one.

The Mosaic law (the law God gave through Moses, which we see in Deuteronomy and Leviticus) provided God's people with the outline for a gracious and just society. These laws were not arbitrary; they set Israel apart in an age of oppression and violence. Not only were the people of Israel called to treat one another with fairness and consideration, they were even called to go above and beyond simple fairness, such as during the seventh-year cancellation of debts (Deuteronomy 15) or the fifty-year Jubilee (Leviticus 25). In the previously noted article, Tim Keller quoted scholar Craig Blomberg on this subject: "Out of love of God and love of neighbor, 'The righteous (*saddiq*) are willing to disadvantage themselves to advantage the community; the wicked are willing to disadvantage the community to advantage themselves.'"[9]

God "disadvantaged" Himself to the utmost when He sent Christ on our behalves. The gospel is the ultimate working of justice for an unjust and undeserving people. Some Christians are tempted to stop here and move no further, but God's incredible justice at the cross is not where He stops—and it's not a place to lie down. The justice of the gospel motivates us to defend the widow and orphan (James 1:27), to do right by the foreigner (Exodus 22:21–24), and to do justice for the weak, afflicted, and destitute (Psalm 82:3).

Some believers think the best way to accomplish this is through changing existing government systems. Others believe justice should be accomplished through personal efforts, fundraising, and church outreach. Whatever form it takes, we can all claim this truth: God is just, and His justice is active, not passive. As part of His body, we must be active too.

God Is Omnipotent

A few years ago the Marvel Universe produced a new show centered on the character of Loki, a mischievous god who consistently makes trouble and walks the line between good and evil. In the show, Loki finds out that his entire life—as well as the lives of every other creature in the movie—has been planned by the Time Keepers. The Time Keepers are in turn commanded by a God-type character who dictates exactly how each life should play out. From birth to death, all decisions must be planned, and anyone who strays from the plan is "pruned."

When the show emerged on the cultural scene, some Christians were bothered by how it presented "God." Was this sovereign God-character a representative of the Christian God? Was this show somehow mocking the Creator? To answer these questions you have to know what the Bible says about God's sovereignty, or omnipotence.

The word *omnipotent* isn't found in the Bible, but this term describes the biblical value of God's all-powerful nature. The word comes from two Latin roots—*omnis* (all) and *potens* (power). In other words, God is all-powerful. When this attribute is expressed over creation, we say that God is *sovereign*.

Scholar Wayne Grudem described omnipotence as God's ability to do "all His holy will."[10] This definition is important because it's not the same as saying "God can do anything." There *are* certain things God cannot do—things that deny His nature! For example:

- God cannot lie (Hebrews 6:18).
- God cannot stop being God (2 Timothy 2:13).
- God cannot tempt us to do evil (James 1:13).

All of these things would require God to deny His perfection, power, or purity. Therefore, God is able to do anything consistent with His character and unable to do things that deny who He is. This "inability" is a form of self-restraint; His holiness restrains Him from doing evil.

Where does the Bible teach about God's power and sovereignty? Many places, but here are a few:

- "Great is our Lord, and abundant in power; his understanding is beyond measure" (Psalm 147:5 ESV).
- "Ah, Lord God! It is you who have made the heavens and the earth by your great power and by your outstretched arm! Nothing is too hard for you" (Jeremiah 32:17 ESV).
- "For behold, he who forms the mountains and creates the wind, and declares to man what is his thought, who makes the morning darkness, and treads on the heights of the earth— the Lord, the God of hosts, is his name!" (Amos 4:13 ESV).
- "For his invisible attributes, namely, his eternal power and divine nature, have been clearly perceived, ever since the creation of the world, in the things that have been made" (Romans 1:20 ESV).
- "He is the radiance of the glory of God and the exact imprint of his nature, and he upholds the universe by the word of his power" (Hebrews 1:3 ESV).
- "Jesus looked at them and said, 'With man this is impossible, but with God all things are possible'" (Matthew 19:26 ESV).

Sometimes Christians misunderstand God's sovereignty. They assume it doesn't matter what we do or how we live; God's will is going to happen anyway. This results in a fatalistic "faith": *Who cares what I do or how I live? God's just going to do what He's going to do.*

But this misconstrues God's omnipotent nature. While God can work His will any way He likes, He permits consequences for our sinful choices. God created humanity with a will, which means we can choose "life or death" (Deuteronomy 30:19). When we choose to live sinfully, we are rejecting God's *perfect will*. As a result, God may delay or alter His perfect, original plan in order to teach us and draw us back to Him. This does not downplay God's sovereignty because He is the one who created humans, gave them a will, and watches over their coming and going (Psalm 121).

There are a variety of views of God's omnipotence. One of these is *determinism*. Determinism falls on a spectrum, with some people saying God causes all things except sin (though He may cause things such as disease and disaster) and others playing the idea out to the logical conclusion—that God is the *author* of evil. Most Calvinistic denominations hold to some form of determinism, though not to the extreme of God authoring evil. The show *Loki* is an example of hyper-determinism: a world in which God is planning the actions of His creatures, whether that be birth, death, salvation, or any life experience.

There is an alternative view, one upheld by classical Arminianism, orthodox Wesleyanism, and other traditions. This view is often summed up as *free will*, but that's really not a great definition. Both Calvinists and Arminians believe in a form of human free will in conjunction with God's sovereignty. A better term for the non-Calvinist approach is *libertarian freedom*.

In this view, God's decision to create people who make free choices does not downplay His sovereignty but rather affirms it. This means that the evil we see in the world is *permitted* by God's sovereign nature because He created people with libertarian free-dom. It is not His *perfect* will for evil to occur, but His *permitted* will, because relationship requires choice. God did not desire the world to have such evil, but in order for humanity to have the freedom of choice and relationship, they have to have the freedom to choose to move away from Him. That's exactly what happened. The Enemy is *permitted* to roam the earth tempting humanity until final judgment (2 Corinthians 4:4; 1 John 5:19; Ephesians 2:2; Revelation 19), and each person will answer for whether she follows Satan or follows Christ.

Christians may come to different conclusions on *how* God's sovereignty operates—determinism or libertarian free will—but what they agree upon is that God *is* the sovereign, reigning authority in this world, and that His creative, loving, gracious power is the anchor of our saving grace. Unlike the "god" of Loki, ours does not prune those who fail to keep to His plan. He offers salvation and redemption.

God Is Omniscient

As I grew into an older teen, still carrying out my secret battle with erotica, I began to question why God had allowed me to stumble upon the book that started it all. *It isn't fair,* I thought. *I was just a kid. I didn't mean it. Sure, what I did with it was wrong, but why did God allow me to find the book at all? If He knows everything, why didn't He do something?*

I think every human asks this question at some point. Maybe you had an alcoholic parent, and it opened the door to your own struggle with addiction. Perhaps you were abused. Maybe you face a painful autoimmune disease. At some point we have to reckon with the biblical truth of an all-knowing, omniscient God who also permits bad things to happen. How do we reconcile these realities? I had to wrestle with this question myself.

God's *omniscience* is His ability to know all things past, present, and future. He is all-knowing. Not only does He know what

37

has happened and what *will* occur, He also knows what could have *possibly* occurred. In Scripture, God's knowledge of the future is described as "foreknowledge," or "perceiving beforehand" (1 Peter 1:2; Acts 2:23). All Christians agree that God is omniscient, but there are varying interpretations of how God's all-knowing nature works out in real life.

Determinism

The determinist view, found often in Calvinistic churches, closely binds foreknowledge with *fore-ordination*. It states that God knows what will happen because He *decreed* it to happen. Determinists believe humans cannot make completely free, libertarian choices because that ability would contradict God's all-knowing, sovereign nature. All things that occur in the world are the product of God's specific decree (order), caused by Him for His purposes. Many determinist scholars argue that God's decrees, while encompassing evil, always work evil for good. In the end, He restores all things, and the things He caused were for His glory.

Open Theism

Determinism is not the only view of how God's knowledge of the future works, though. The *open theism* view says that God restrains His foreknowledge and does not actually know some things, such as who will choose to follow Him. It can be expressed this way: God knows everything that *can* be known, and some things—like future human choices—cannot be known.

While appealing, the open theism view has a very difficult time upholding the character of a truly sovereign God. It also contradicts Scripture's teaching that God knows all things that have been and will be:

- "Great is our LORD, and abundant in power; his understanding is beyond measure" (Psalm 147:5 ESV).

- "For whenever our heart condemns us, God is greater than our heart, and he knows everything" (1 John 3:20 ESV).
- "And you, Solomon my son, know the God of your father and serve him with a whole heart and with a willing mind, for the LORD searches all hearts and understands every plan and thought. If you seek him, he will be found by you, but if you forsake him, he will cast you off forever" (1 Chronicles 28:9 ESV).
- "Oh, the depth of the riches and wisdom and knowledge of God! How unsearchable are his judgments and how inscrutable his ways! 'For who has known the mind of the Lord, or who has been his counselor? Or who has given a gift to him that he might be repaid?' For from him and through him and to him are all things" (Romans 11:33–36 ESV).
- "Who has measured the Spirit of the LORD, or what man shows him his counsel? Whom did he consult, and who made him understand? Who taught him the path of justice, and taught him knowledge, and showed him the way of understanding?" (Isaiah 40:13–14 ESV).

Molinism

A third approach to God's omniscience is Molinism. It strikes a bit of a balance between determinism and open theism. To summarize their belief: God knows all choices that will be made and works through those free choices to accomplish His purposes. Molinism teaches that God has a "middle knowledge" of what choices humans *will* make, and He chooses to permit those choices and work through them to accomplish His purposes.

Some theologians say that Arminians (those who hold to libertarian freedom) are Molinists. Others argue that Molinism leans toward determinism, because God places people in circumstances where their choices will inevitably be what His "middle knowledge" has foreknown. The classical Arminian view, though similar to Molinism in many ways, differs slightly. It upholds the absolute omniscience of God—knowing past, present, future, and all possibilities. It also upholds the libertarian freedom of humans. God knows what people will choose, but He does not cause them to choose it. God's Spirit is involved in convicting, leading, and counseling people in their decisions.

As I struggled to understand how God could know my future and yet permit it, I came to realize that the only way to understand God's foreknowledge was to also understand His love. For me to experience God's gracious love, I had to both *know my need for Him* and *recognize the nature of this world*. I encountered pornography because the world is a broken and dark place. God did not desire that I encounter it or wish for me to experience that darkness. But He permitted it and my free choices within it in order to provide me a chance at a relationship with Him. God knew I would face the darkness. And He knew that in the darkness I would find His Light.

Today, I have had the privilege of sharing God's hope with hundreds of women who are getting free from sexual sin. I asked God "Why?" at the time; today I think I know why, or at least part of the reason. God's glory and goodness have been displayed through the painful, lonely, dark time of my teens and twenties. He knew it would happen. He did not cause it. But He did cause many to know His love because of it.

The Ocean of God

Knowing and believing God's love began my journey to freedom from porn. But the greater gift I received was a deeper, sweeter relationship with the Father. I no longer looked at Him as an unkind and distant judge. I understood God's love in a new way—how His love was expressed through justice and holiness, and how that was for my *good*. God's hatred of sin was not a threat to me; it was the guarantor of my safety. He was on the side of my freedom. He was, and is, *for me*. This reframing of God's character enabled me to fight my addiction to sexual sin not from fear or guilt but from an identity as a loved child of God.

In the ocean of God's character, we've only dipped our toes into a tide pool. There are so many attributes we did not cover in this chapter—so many I wish I could include! As you continue your study of the Father, keep His unity front and center. He is not different in character from Christ and the Spirit. They are *One*: all loving, all just, all holy, all powerful—*together*. Splitting them apart into the pieces we find most comfortable or approachable is a path to confusion, or worse, false teaching about God.

It takes some wrestling to reckon with the texts about God, but when we understand the Bible as a cohesive narrative and Jesus as the very Son of God, proceeding from the Father who loves us and sent His Son to reveal such love (John 3:16), we discover a depth of relationship with Him we had missed before. God must be taken together with all His attributes; after all, He has given all of Himself to be known and loved, and everything He did through the gospel made it possible for you to experience that relationship.

GOD'S GLORY AND GOODNESS

If you read a lot of Christian books, you'll hear a good bit about God's "glory." We say our actions "glorify God" or that nature "displays God's glory." God's glory can be described as His majesty or His awesomeness. But we see God define it for us in Exodus 33. In this passage,

Moses met with God and begged to see God's glory. God responded, "I will cause all my goodness to pass in front of you, and I will proclaim my name, the LORD, in your presence" (v. 19). God's glory is God's goodness! When the Bible talks about glorifying God, it's not saying God is an attention-seeking megalomaniac. God wants His glory to be visible because His glory is His goodness. And when God's goodness is on display, His love and kindness bless the world.

Chapter 3

Cosmology: A Beautiful, Broken World

THE DOCTRINES OF CREATION, HUMANITY, AND SIN

If you spend enough time around small children, you'll hear echoes of your own questions in theirs. In the nighttime, with curtains drawn in the pink bedroom and a blinking star night-light wobbling on the hamper, kids become tiny philosophers. "Why was I born? Who made the stars? Why do bad things happen to good people?"

In our family, we homeschool and run a home-based business. Josh and I are with three children under six almost every hour of the day. Our worlds are melded to our children's, and this constant exposure grants us front-row seats to what goes through those little minds. When our six-year-old told us how Dr. Binocs (a character from a favorite kids TV show) had explained the human descent from apes, she wanted to know how the show lined up with the story of God's creation we'd been teaching her since babyhood. At *six years old* she was asking a question scientists and theologians have wrestled with for years.

The questions our children are asking are the questions we as grown women should be asking as well. Unfortunately, as distracted, busy adults, we often get too wrapped up in the daily grind to deal with things like cosmology. In fact, most of us don't stop to really think about it until we have someone else asking us to explain! And while I can't promise to answer every question you have, I hope you'll come away from this chapter with a better foundation for understanding God and the world He created.

What Is Cosmology?

Cosmology is the study of the origin and purpose of the universe. It is not a strictly Christian discipline; secular scientists and philosophers also study cosmology. In the last few centuries, particularly since Darwin's theory of evolution was introduced, secular cosmology has increasingly separated from religion.

COSMOLOGY: *the study of the origin and purpose of the universe*

But the Christian religion, by nature, can never be separated from cosmology. Because Christians believe in a creating God, we view the world as a sovereignly structured entity. We wrestle with questions of origin, the meaning of life, and what happens after death because the Bible speaks to all these things. Christians should have an opinion on cosmology because Christianity deals in the subject at length.

The *Stanford Encyclopedia of Philosophy* sums it up this way: "[According to theists] the world only exists because of an ultimate and supernatural cause which is, as Newton said, 'not blind and fortuitous, but very well skilled in Mechanicks and Geometry.'

Whether in a general philosophical sense
or in a scientific sense, cosmology has
always been part of theism."[1] All three
theistic religions—Islam, Judaism, and
Christianity—are inherently cosmological.
They make claims about the origin, meaning, and destiny of the world. Though
there are varying stances on how science

THEISM: *a belief in a*
god or a creator who
is personally involved
in his creation

and religion are synthesized, there is no question that the Bible, in
particular, speaks to the purpose of the universe. It wrestles with
the questions of life and death and ultimately answers them in the
Person of God:

> [The] creation cosmology as revealed in the Bible (Genesis 1–2)
> [is] God created the universe and created people in His image to
> have a relationship with Him. History is moving to a final cli-
> max that He has ordained. Everything has purpose and meaning
> because God gives it purpose and meaning. Even in cultures that
> do not have (or believe) the Genesis account, a supernatural expla-
> nation to the origin of the world is still apparent.[2]

This view of the world as a purposeful, richly endowed creation
is not comfortable for some. Such a Creator requires accountability.
If there is a moral Lawgiver whose law disagrees with the morphing
desires of human hearts, we have to answer to Him. We have to
align our plans, desires, and views of the world with His existence.
This changes the standard of morality from subjective—defined by
me and my feelings—to objective, defined by the God who made me.

In *The Magician's Nephew*, the first in C. S. Lewis's famous
Chronicles of Narnia series, the creation of the world is described
in ardent detail. If you're familiar with the book, you'll remember
the scene where Digory and Polly (the main characters) are dumped
into an "empty world."[3] It is completely dark and silent. And then,

breaking through the void, comes a voice. Aslan, the great lion of Narnia, sings the world into existence:

> The sky, in that one place, grew slowly and steadily paler. You could see shapes of hills standing up dark against it. All the time the Voice went on singing . . . The eastern sky changed from white to pink and from pink to gold. The Voice rose and rose, till all the air was shaking with it. And just as it swelled to the mightiest and most glorious sound it had yet produced, the sun arose.[4]

This picture of an intentional, beautiful world, created with joy and singing for the purpose of beauty and love, is what we see in the Bible itself. Lewis wrote these themes into children's stories because he believed the Creator, the moral Lawgiver, to be essential to correct cosmology. Everything we believe about the world, humanity, life, and godliness begins with the One who created it all.

Christian cosmology opens our eyes and hearts to the magnificent intentionality of the universe—and our purpose within it.

The Beautiful, Broken Creation

Adeline was frustrated. She snipped, turned, bent the scissors as best she could, irritation building at each turn. Trying to cut around a curve in the pattern of her paper, she snipped off an important part of her piece.

Having left the room for a moment, I returned to find an empty seat, scattered papers, and no Adeline.

"Adeline?" I called. "Where are you? What happened?"

"I don't want to do it," a small voice replied, muffled by the cardboard box from whence it emerged.

"But it's okay if it isn't perfect," I said, examining the paper.

"You can try again!" A small hand reached out from the box and tossed a piece of blue construction paper at my feet. Cardboard "doors" slammed shut. I picked up the paper. Depicted in bold strokes was a drawing of a table covered in crafting supplies, with a vibrantly colored girl holding scissors and looking very . . . well, blue. In more ways than one.

"What's this?"

"It's a picture of me messing up my picture," replied the voice. Indeed it was—a drawing of Adeline creating imperfect art, scowling eyebrows darkening the cartoon face. I covered my chuckle; the resemblance was true.

"Honey," I cracked open the cardboard doors. "Nothing we create will ever be perfect! It's okay to mess it up. *Let's try again.*"

Christian cosmology starts out with the beauty of Genesis 1 and 2: "In the beginning God created . . ." (Genesis 1:1). He began it all by pouring Himself, His heart, His voice into a void and calling forth beauty from darkness. What perfect balance! What excellence and order!

But the beauty didn't last long. In Genesis 3, the beautiful world was broken:

> The serpent was more crafty than any of the wild animals the LORD God had made. He said to the woman, "Did God really say, 'You must not eat from any tree in the garden'?" The woman said to the serpent, "We may eat fruit from the trees in the garden, but God did say, 'You must not eat fruit from the tree that is in the middle of the garden, and you must not touch it, or you will die.'" "You will not certainly die," the serpent said to the woman. "For God knows that when you eat from it your eyes will be opened, and you will be like God, knowing good and evil." (vv. 1–5)

The first humans chose to believe an Accuser instead of their Creator. The consequence was the loss of perfect unity with God,

ANTHROPOLOGY: *the study of humanity's origin, nature, and destiny*

HAMARTIOLOGY: *the study of sin's definition, effects, and redemption*

making it impossible to dwell in His presence without shame. The beautiful world was broken by sin.

To fully grasp our purpose in the world as it exists today, we have to reckon with the sin that marred it. We can never be the perfect creation of Genesis 1 again. Until God reconciles all things, we are impacted by the imperfection of sin. Anything we create is an echo of God's creativity and innovation, but it won't be perfect. Nothing will be.

Where does this lead us? We have to deal with two other "ologies": *anthropology*, the study of humanity's origin, nature, and destiny; and *hamartiology*, the study of sin's definition, effects, and redemption. To do this, we will explore more deeply God, humans, and sin. As we go along, we'll answer some big questions:

- Why did God create the world?
- What does it mean that God is Creator?
- How does that impact my daily life?

We'll also answer some more nuanced questions:

- If God created the world, how did He do it? How do I understand Genesis 1–2?
- How do I view science in light of my Christian faith?
- What did Christians believe about God as Creator in past centuries?

We will start with that last question because it gives guidance to the others.

The Church Fathers on Creator God

Picture church history like a family tree. There's you, a little face at the bottom. Above you is the trunk of a great oak. This is Christ. Branching out from Him are hundreds and thousands of faces, some familiar, some not. Your great, great, great, great-times-ten grandfathers of the faith are whom we call the early church fathers. These are the bishops and pastors who ministered shortly after the apostles (within the first five hundred years after Jesus' ministry). We look to them for guidance on topics in Scripture because they give us a peek at how the church operated in its early years. They show us what doctrines were essential to Christianity, what behaviors were considered evidence of Christian life, and what things were important but not worth dividing the church over.

Creation is one doctrine the early church talked about on a frequent basis. The early pastors believed God's creative identity was inextricably linked to His triune nature (Father, Spirit, and Son).

Church father Irenaeus put it this way in his work *Against Heresies*:

> In this way, then, it is demonstrated [that there is] One God, [the] Father, uncreated, invisible, Creator of all, above whom there is no other God, and after whom there is no other God. And as God is verbal, therefore, He made created things by the Word [Jesus]; and God is Spirit, so that He adorned all things by the Spirit. . . . Thus, since the Word [Jesus] "establishes," that is, works bodily and confers existence, while the Spirit arranges and forms the various "powers," so rightly is the Son called the Word and the Spirit the Wisdom of God.[5]

Irenaeus was saying that God, through His powerful Word (another name for Christ), established and gave existence to the world. All other beliefs about God, Christ, and humanity rely upon this foundational truth.

According to Athanasius, another early church father, the creation of the world by the triune God—a work of Father, Spirit, and Son—was the first step in a redemption narrative that Christ made complete.[6]

Clearly the early church fathers didn't have the scientific perspective we do today. They had never heard Darwin's theory of evolution. Even so, they still had to defend their view of an intelligent Creator to the people of their day. A Creator-less theory of existence had already been proposed among Greek philosophers.

Athanasius and other church fathers contradicted the Epicurean philosophers by arguing for an intentional, loving Creator. And while the early fathers agreed that God initiated the universe, early pastors like Augustine, Justin Martyr, Clement, and Origen had varied views on *how* God created the world and how long it took Him. Even today, theologians are divided on how God chose to create the world.

Theories of Creation

Maybe you've heard of the multiple ways Christians approach the creation story. Some believe in a literal six-day creation as described in Genesis 1 and 2; they are called "young earth creationists." Biologists, geneticists, and other scientists have made a case for the literal interpretation of these verses and the possibility of their scientific accuracy.

Other theologians and Christian scientists (especially geologists) disagree, saying the Hebrew word *yom* translated as "day" in Genesis 1 does not always mean a twenty-four-hour day; it can refer to a longer period of time. These believers propose "day age" creation, which suggests that each "day" of creation was actually an era of time. As a result, those who hold this view are often called "old earth creationists." This theory attempts to reconcile a creating God with modern scientists' estimated age of the earth.

Gap theory holds to a literal six-day creation *after* eons of time.

Adherents to this view believe there is a "gap" between Genesis 1:1 ("God created the heavens and the earth") and Genesis 1:2 ("the earth was formless and empty"). To gap theorists, this gap of time explains scientists' estimated age of the earth. The gap theory first emerged in the seventeenth century to explain the fall of Satan. Some theologians believed Satan's fall may have occurred in the "gap" between verses 1 and 2. However, Hebrew scholars argue that the grammar in Genesis 1 doesn't support this view.[7]

A fourth view, sometimes combined with a modified gap theory, is theistic evolution. As the name indicates, proponents of this view believe God used evolution to accomplish His creative purposes. Theistic evolutionists believe that the fall of humanity resulted in only *human death*, not plant or animal death, and that plant or animal death was permitted by God to accomplish His creative purposes. The biggest biblical stumbling block with this view is that its timeline has death occurring before sin, since evolution requires death (through natural selection) to develop a new species. Scripture indicates that God's creation did not *require* death; it was anti-death. Sin had to be present for death to occur (Genesis 3–4).

Theistic evolutionists generally believe the intent of Genesis 1 and 2 was not to depict a scientific play-by-play of creation, because the ancient people it was written to would not have read it with such a lens. The disagreement between the biblical narrative and evolutionary narrative is not as disturbing to theistic evolutionists as it would be to Christians adhering to other creation theories.

Each of these creation theories has its weaknesses—some scientifical, some biblical. The passages about creation were written thousands of years ago in a different time. This doesn't make the creation narrative any less trustworthy for teaching us about God today, but it should make us scientifically inquisitive: How does God reveal Himself in the physical world? As we study the varied views of this topic, we should keep in mind the respective bias of those speaking as well as the problems that arise from holding such a view. This kind of comparison and testing is not an expression of doubt and should not be shamed; it is a form of critical thinking that helps us form an educated and biblical faith.

As we consider different creation theories, we must remember the consistent core doctrine we see in Scripture and church history: God created the world. He not only was there at the beginning, He *is* the beginning: "I am the Alpha and the Omega, the First and the Last, the Beginning and the End" (Revelation 22:13).

Humanity: The Created Image of God

The early church fathers believed that God's identity as Creator was the starting point for understanding human identity. This helps us answer the questions of anthropology: How did we get here? Who are we? Where are we going?

The Bible tells us God created humans "a little lower than the angels" (Psalm 8:5) and "in his own image" (Genesis 1:27–28). Scholars have debated what it means that God made us in His image. It could mean we have the capacity to reason, the possession of free will, and the ability to think and to love. These all are part of the answer—but there must be more to it, because we know that those who are unable to exercise reason or free will (such as the unborn or those with intellectual disabilities) are still made in the image of God.

The word *image* is referring not just to something within humanity but to *the pattern in which a human is made.*[8] Humans carry the essence of what they represent—God. At the time Genesis 1 through 3 was written, the authors understood *image* in the same way we understand *idol*. An image represents, and is a likeness of, the god or king after which it is formed. In pagan religions such images are worshiped. In the biblical narrative, the "idols" of the one true God are not made of stone or wood but of human flesh. We are the idols of God. We are His image on earth. This is one of the reasons idolatry is so offensive to the God of the Bible. Why would the images of God worship another image?

Eighteenth-century pastor John Wesley said that sin marred the image of God in humanity but did not destroy the image completely. To be human is to bear God's image; the divine imprint cannot be fully removed from a human being, even by sin. Our humanity exists and is utterly bound up in the sustaining existence of God. This inherent, inalienable image attributes value to every human life.

This is why murder, abortion, and hatred are all against God's laws (Exodus 20:13; Matthew 5:21–22; 1 John 3:15). This is why racism, favoritism, and bigotry are also condemned by the Lord (James 2:8–9, Acts 10:34–36). Humans are unlike any other living creature. They bear the mark of God, a spirit breathed alive by His power. To hate, wound, or kill an image bearer of God is an offense against God Himself.

Because of sin, this image in humanity is marred and broken, but it is still there. In Christ, the fullness of that image is restored. Christ is the full and complete image of God, and that tells us something about who we are and who we become in Him. It points us to the truth that we were created to know God, to be and act like Him.

In Genesis 1 and 2 we see humanity made in God's "image" or "likeness," as idols on earth. In Genesis 5:3, the same word translated as "image" or "likeness" is used to describe Seth as Adam's son. Humans image God both as idols (spiritual representatives) and children (loved creations). According to the IVP Old Testament commentary, we do that through the tools of conscience, self-awareness, and spiritual discernment.[9]

Did God Set Us Up for Failure?

Adam and Eve's first mission was to care for the world (Genesis 2:15). They were free to enjoy the garden as they labored, eating from whatever tree they wished—except for one. They were forbidden from eating of the Tree of Knowledge of Good and Evil, and disobedience bore a heavy price: death.

Was God unreasonable?

"Why would God create humans who don't know right and wrong and put them in a position to make a moral choice?" This question came into my inbox, and I chewed on it, cursor blinking. I understood the question, and I found myself asking more: Was God unreasonable? Is that what God was doing in the garden of Eden—creating an impossible dilemma, setting humans up for failure? If so, it would be difficult to believe God is actually good.

It's right to ask the hard questions of Scripture. It's good to employ our minds in pursuit of truth, even when the questions are uncomfortable and risky. If we're going to discuss the image of God in humans, we have to discuss humanity's ability to respond to God in the first place.

Let's look again at the one command God gave Adam and Eve: *Don't eat of the Tree of Knowledge of Good and Evil.* Keep in mind that the "knowledge of good and evil" does not mean "mental awareness of good and evil." They certainly had this; it was an ability imbued by their Creator. They knew right from wrong because God outlined it for them:

> The LORD God took the man and put him in the Garden of Eden to work it and take care of it. And the LORD God commanded the man, "You are free to eat from any tree in the garden; but you must not eat from the tree of the knowledge of good and evil, for when you eat from it you will certainly die." (Genesis 2:15–17)

Adam and Eve knew, intellectually, *about* evil. But they had not experienced it. Their disobedience opened them to the full, intimate experience of evil, something from which God was protecting them. Others believe it may be that the "knowledge of good and evil" was "the desire to *determine* good and evil"—to take God's role for themselves. In both interpretations, humanity rejects God's protection and sovereignty and invites sin into the world.

This remains the struggle we face today. Will we accept God's protection and trust His will, or will we create our own moral guidelines? The fall of humanity at the beginning of time remains the fall we take every day since.

Sin: The Creation Destroyer

Winter lasts six months in northern Michigan. From the end of October to April, the winds gale from the west, snow falls in pristine drifts, and we build toasty fires to outlast it all. Hunkered down after our little kids go to bed, Josh and I seek whatever indoor date-night activities we can find. We were delighted when a couple at our church started an axe-throwing company in our Michigan town. The first time we went, the owner walked us through the details of how to throw an axe of varied weight so we'd be more likely to hit the target.

During my first few tries I blushed red. I hit every part of the wall except the target: right side, left side, top, bottom. The axe bounced from wooden wall to rubber floor with terrifying alacrity. I would have made a terrible Viking and an even worse lumberjack. Eventually, I found a groove; the axe started landing squarely in the target, spinning through the air, slicing the wooden wall. With a resounding *thump* it stuck to the bull's-eye.

Sin has been defined as missing the mark (1 John 3:4). Like an axe bouncing off the wall and dangerously spinning back toward the thrower, sin damages all that it touches. Sin undoes the creation of beauty, order, and peace; it is ugliness, disorder, and chaos. According to Genesis 3, sin entered when the first humans chose to reject God's command (one intended for their well-being and protection) and determine morality for themselves. Their distrust and rebellion changed the human world for all their descendants.

This was not, however, how sin entered the universe as a whole. Before Adam and Eve were created, the biblical accounts indicate that another "order" of beings rebelled against God's perfection and introduced sin into creation. It is one of these beings, the Serpent, or Accuser, who tempted the man and woman to follow his path. Theologian Dr. J. Oliver Buswell Jr. described the origin of sin as "an act of free will in which the creature deliberately, responsibly, and with adequate understanding of the issues chose to corrupt the holy character of godliness with which God had endowed his creation."[10]

Corruption impacts everything. Though the sin of Satan (a name that means "adversary") was originally confined to the angelic realm, Adam and Eve's willful choice to align with him brought sin into the realm of humanity. As humans became increasingly evil, God revealed more and more of Himself and His law.

Over the course of the Bible, we gain clarity on what constitutes sin. More than just missing the mark, sin is described in the Bible as transgression of the law of God (1 John 3:4) and rebellion against God (Deuteronomy 9:7; Joshua 1:18). Sin is anything that does not spring from a faith-transformed heart (Romans 14:23). The apostle James said that if we know the good we *ought* to do and don't do it, that is sin (James 4:17). This "sense of oughtness," or conscience, is innate to human beings—and "the mere fact that we have a sense of what ought, or ought not, to be . . . is inexplicable."[11]

As I write I look out my office window to the backyard of our farm. Within vision is a thirty-foot walnut tree, lean and brown, branches stretching toward the barn and fields. It's a beautiful tree; the squirrels love it as much as I do. But what you wouldn't know from a cursory glance is that this tree is poisonous to most garden plants. When we first moved to the farm and I chose a spot for my garden, I was crushed to discover anything we planted near the walnut tree could die from the toxic roots underground. To protect the plants, we distanced our garden from the tree and built raised beds to keep them away from the underground poison.

Sin is like the walnut tree. Even the smallest amount corrupts and destroys the possibility of perfection, of growth. Its impact is far-reaching, poisoning the things planted upon it. It seems so harmless to be the source of one's own authority, to determine good for ourselves. That's the lie our Adamic ancestors believed. However, the introduction of sin into the world was not God's perfect desire for humans. Although He foresaw it, He did not cause it. He did not plan it. He risked it.

For humanity to experience love, they had to be free. God risked everything in permitting this freedom. It was a freedom authored and bestowed by His own hand, a power of choice that could result in mutual love or rebellious resistance. "No man sins because he has not grace but because he does not use the grace which he hath," said John Wesley, and it is true.[12] God's grace gave humanity the freedom to choose. And God's grace permits that choice today.

Unlike Satan, humanity is salvable. From the moment of humanity's first sinful choice, God set in motion a promise to redeem, restore, and make all things new. Sin's power has an expiration date.

The Poison of Original Sin

After moving our garden away from the walnut tree and building eight raised beds, I ordered a dump truck of soil to fill them. *All I need is dirt, water, sun, and seeds—right?* I filled the beds with the soil, wheeled barrows of manure from our rabbits and pigs, and eagerly planted my seeds. But by early summer, my cucumbers were struggling. Cucumbers are very easy to grow; I felt foolish. What could be the problem?

The cucumbers struggled on. By midsummer they were still small and sickly, but they had produced a little fruit. I was so excited to serve them to guests. I checked them daily, watering and weeding, measuring their size. Finally came the harvest. As I chopped them for a salad, I popped a slice into my mouth. *Gag!* The bitterness stung my mouth, wrapping an aftertaste around my tongue. We could never serve those to friends! Determined to find out why my cucumbers had failed, I learned that nutrient-deprived soil results in bitter fruit. The soil in my garden looked fine, but it could not produce good vegetables.

All humanity was affected by Adam and Eve's ethical decision to choose rebellion over righteousness. Like the soil in my garden, imperfection cannot grow perfection. Every person born is affected by sin, and it is from the effects of this predisposition that we need to be saved.

Original sin, and the need for salvation from it, is a core teaching of Christianity and has been from the beginning. However, scholars differ on *how* original sin works. There are a few different views of it, but we will look at two.

- *Federal original sin*: This view holds that Adam was the "head" of the human race, and as such, our representative. Because of his sin, we, the members of his family, are also affected by sin. This is called *imputed sin*. Other scholars hold to a "seminal" or biological view—sin is transmitted genetically, and we inherit it because we are Adam's biological descendants (Romans 5:12, 19). This is called *inherited sin*. Many Christians adhere to both views under the umbrella of federal original sin.
- *Predisposed original sin*: This view holds that each person is born with a predisposition to sin but is not condemned, or separated from God, until that person acts upon it with willful rebellion. This predisposition is the product of being born into a sin-affected race and world. In this view, each person is "bent" toward sin but is not held responsible for what Adam did; they are only responsible for their own sins.

The Augsburg Confession, a statement of faith from the Lutheran Church in 1530, described the effects of original sin this way: it caused humanity to be "without the fear of God and without trust in Him, and with concupiscence [evil desire]; and this disease or original fault is truly sin, condemning and bringing eternal death now also upon all that are not born again by baptism and the Holy Spirit."[13]

In other words: Original sin makes us hostile to God. We need someone to bridge the gaping ravine between us and our Creator.

The good news? That Someone is Jesus Christ!

We have a separate chapter outlining what Jesus did with sin and how that impacts us because it's a big story that deserves its own airtime. But the good news really is good news: Jesus rights the wrongs of sin in the world. He is justice, peace, kindness, and rest. He is, as John Piper put it, "our hope":

Once sin entered the world and everything was corrupted, and once God's saving purposes began to rescue people from sin, the glorious and beautiful purposes of this creation were thrust forward into the time when Christ would come again and set everything right: a time of perfect righteousness, a time of perfect peace, a new creation with no crying or pain anymore, so that over and over again in the Scriptures we are told to rejoice in hope—like Romans 5:2: "Rejoice in hope of the glory of God."[14]

In a world groaning beneath the weight of sin (Romans 8:22), we rejoice in *hope* that Christ came not just to save us eternally and restore us to God but to restore *all things*. Every injustice wrought by sin's evil effects will be brought to account. Every evil thought, deed, and disease will answer for what it did to humanity, God's beloved image bearers. And ultimately Satan, the Accuser, will answer for it as well (Revelation 20). But we'll get to that at the end of this book.

Thou, Be Sure, Shall Give Account

Famous atheist Bertrand Russell once described his perspective on existence in an incredibly bleak way:

> No fire, no heroism, no intensity of thought and feeling, can preserve an individual life beyond the grave; that all the labours of the ages, all the devotion, all the inspiration, all the noonday brightness of human genius, are destined to extinction in the vast death of the solar system, and . . . the whole temple of Man's achievement must inevitably be buried beneath the debris of a universe in ruins.[15]

Look about you. We do live amid a "universe in ruins." But running through that universe is a thread of hope, red as blood, hung like the cord in Rahab's window:

Help is on the way.

Salvation is here.

Humans want to be free—often, that means free from the moral obligations a created being has to its Creator. The quote above is from Russell's work *A Free Man's Worship*—but his version of freedom is a hopeless one. It encompassed only the freedom to attempt sovereignty on his own terms. Christians have a much greater, truer freedom: we are free within the safety of a God who loves and saves us from the thing that destroys. In this beautiful, broken world, we get to choose whether we align with hope or with hopelessness. Both offer a form of freedom, but only one of those freedoms redeems.

In John Milton's famous poem, *Paradise Lost*, there is an extensive dialogue between Satan and several angels. The angel Zephon challenges Satan:

> Thou, be sure, shalt give account
> To him who sent us, whose charge is to keep
> This place inviolable, and these from harm.

Satan's response to Zephon's rebuke is described by Milton:

> Abashed the Devil stood,
> And felt how awful goodness is, and saw
> Virtue in her shape how lovely—saw, and pined
> His loss . . .[16]

The goodness of God is indeed "awe-full"—full of awe, beauty, and power. It is so powerful it made Satan lose. And like Milton described in his poem, Satan knows the "awful goodness" of God and is extremely aware of his loss. Though he has been given a time of temporary earthly "reign," the long-term power of his evil is broken. He will give account to the One who "keeps [us] from harm"! This world may be broken and experiencing evil, but it is being restored, and the groaning universe will one day receive its justice at last.

But there's still a bit of theology between now and then, and it all begins with the Suffering King.

WHAT MAKES HUMANS SPECIAL?

Humans weren't the first beings God created; an entire host of angelic beings were already alive. In fact, some scholars believe that the "us" in Genesis 1:26—"Let us make mankind in our image"—is not referring to the Trinity but is God speaking to the "host of heaven," the witness of angels who watched Him create a new race of people.[17]

So if humans weren't the first beings created, what makes us so special? Why did God need humans if He already had thousands of angels?

Scripture makes a distinction between angels and humans and never states that angels are the image of God like humans are. Humans are material and immaterial—body and soul. Based on how the Bible describes them, angels are spirit beings (Hebrews 1:14) created in a different kingdom, or class, than humans. They are eternal and have a spiritual wisdom and power greater than what humans experience on earth. Humanity is "a little lower than the angels" (Psalm 8:5), and yet angels are sent to serve and help humanity at God's command. The Greek word for angel, *angelos,* means "messenger," and the word is used both for the angelic being and also for the office or task of bearing a message.

For humans to image God differently than angels seems to require a physical body in a material world. This should remind us just how much God cares about our physical bodies (and our physical world!). Our bodies are not less important than our souls; the two are woven together, a means of imaging God in a material universe. Our bodies distinguish us from angels and equip us to be "idols of God" to the world. "Our job on earth is to cultivate the godly side of our nature and integrate it into the earthly side of our nature. Our job is to reveal heaven on earth, and as creatures containing elements of both heaven and earth, we are perfectly suited for the job."[18]

Chapter 4

Christology: And He Dwelt Among Us

THE DOCTRINE OF CHRIST

It took four years of marriage for me to remember my husband's birthday.

Through two years of dating and four years of our marriage, I could not remember whether my husband's birthday was July 14 or July 16. The situation was so dire that Josh temporarily used his birthday as a password just to train me in remembering it (don't do that—it's not secure!). For years I continued to mix up the two days and would find myself frantic on the thirteenth of July as I realized the extra two days I thought I had were not reality.

Perhaps you are judging me for my birthday mix-up; it's deserved. You may wonder how I could know my husband so well and also . . . not at all. It's a valid question (though I have since memorized his birthday). But it's also a question many Christians should be asking about their relationship with Christ.

CHRISTOLOGY:
the study of Christ's character, humanity, deity, and future return

How many of us know Jesus—learning the facts about Him and memorizing verses describing Him and His actions— but don't really *know* him? If we were asked, "Who is Jesus, and what did He do?" could we answer? Or what about this one: "Why do you follow Him?"

Do we know? What would we say?

Christology is the theology of Christ, the study of His character, humanity, deity, and future return. And though whole books have been written on this topic alone, this chapter will endeavor to give a high-level overview of who Jesus is: the who, what, and why of Christology.

What a Bro We Have in Jesus

Bedtime approaches and little feet scramble under covers as we sing a song or two to the children. They get to pick. Sometimes it's "Beauty and the Beast," other times "Twinkle Twinkle Little Star," "As the Deer," or a recent favorite, "What a Friend We Have in Jesus." If you've never heard this hymn, the lyrics are sweet:

> *What a friend we have in Jesus,*
> *all our sins and griefs to bear!*
> *What a privilege to carry*
> *everything to God in prayer!*
> *O what peace we often forfeit,*
> *O what needless pain we bear,*
> *all because we do not carry*
> *everything to God in prayer!*[1]

In the dim light of evening, this little song leads to discussions of Jesus as "friend." What does it mean that Jesus is our friend? How do we view Him as an authority, a king, but also someone who comes alongside and meets us where we are? This tension is what made Jesus' statement of His friendship so powerful: "I no longer call you servants, because a servant does not know his master's business. Instead, I have called you friends, for everything that I learned from my Father I have made known to you" (John 15:15).

Jesus' friendship is a comforting reality. But sometimes we view Him as more of a "bro" than a friend. A "bro" is a yes-man. He agrees with us, he's always down for a party, he'll go where we go (and probably bring a six-pack). A bro never challenges us.

Jesus is not that kind of friend. He loves us, but He's not going to let us make Him small. He is, after all, the "Alpha and the Omega . . . the Beginning and the End" (Revelation 22:13). He is "the image of the invisible God, the firstborn over all creation" (Colossians 1:15). The fact Jesus would call us friends is not a statement about us and our worthiness but a statement about *Him* and His grace.

And that brings us to the main point: we can't effectively trust Jesus and walk with Him if we *don't know who He is*. We might know He lived, died, and rose again. But do we know what He said about His deity? What does it mean that He is both God and man? (That's a little crazy, if we're being honest!) How about His death on the cross—how exactly does that "save" us? And where did He go after that? What's He doing "on high" with God?

These are the questions the skeptics are asking, and while Jesus doesn't shame those of us who come to Him by simple faith, Christian maturity necessitates asking such hard questions *for ourselves*. Finding these answers helps us engage our culture. It also deepens our personal appreciation for and walk with Jesus. Jesus was a nuanced person and there is much we could discuss regarding

His character, so for ease of our study in this chapter we'll look at six key areas:

- Old Testament prophecies about Jesus
- the preexistence of Jesus
- His humanity
- His deity
- His death
- His resurrection

I Told You So: Prophecies About Jesus

In our last chapter we looked at God's good design for the universe and how sin's corruption broke that perfect world. When Adam and Eve invited sin into the human person, they could no longer be at peace with God. They needed a way to dwell with Him at peace.

God chose to reveal Himself to humans through a series of "covenants," or treaties, in which He promised to be faithful and lead His people to be a beacon of hope among the nations. These covenants were time-bound and specific. God chose to work through the specific cultural context of ancient times, including their cultural covenant structure, to express His faithfulness. But these covenants, and the law He graciously gave to Israel (the people who revealed Him to the world) were a shadow of what was to come: Jesus Christ (Colossians 2:17).

- In Eden, God dwelt with humans in perfect love and peace.
- After Eden, God dwelt with Seth, Noah, Abraham, Isaac, and Jacob through specific revelations of Himself in their time.
- When the nation of Israel left Egypt, God dwelt with them in a tabernacle designed with heavenly proportions.

- When Solomon came to the throne of Israel, God left the tabernacle to dwell with Israel in a permanent temple of ornate gold and cedar.

God's goal has always been to restore perfect love and peace between Himself and His creation. Israel operated as a "city on a hill," a light to the nations whose laws allowed them to live in the literal, concentrated presence of God. But even God's beautiful temple, a place for Jews and Gentiles alike to come and worship, could not be preserved from humanity's sin. When Israel rebelled against God and partnered with idolatrous nations, they invited evil into this sacred place. The temple was destroyed, the ark of the covenant stolen, and with it, all hope of God dwelling with humanity.

Until Jesus.

The Old Testament concludes as if all has been lost. Israel went into exile and did not repent of their sinful ways. The prophets went silent for four hundred years. This intertestamental period was a time of war and oppression. Yet during this time of darkness and silence, God was at work. The ancient words of the previous years were throbbing with promise: *the Messiah is coming.*

The Old Testament is littered with prophecies about Jesus' entrance into the world. The authors of the Gospels made an effort to link their accounts to the Old Testament prophets as evidence of Jesus' unique character. Here are a few of the prophecies fulfilled by Jesus' birth:

- Numbers 24:17—He would be from the line of Jacob
- Isaiah 11:1—He would be born from the family of Jesse
- Jeremiah 23:5–6—He would be David's kingly heir
- Micah 5:2—He would be born in Bethlehem
- Isaiah 7:14—He would be immaculately conceived (born of a virgin)

- Psalm 72:10—He would be worshiped and given gifts at His birth
- Jeremiah 31:15—A king would murder children in an attempt to kill Jesus[2]

The prophets spoke of a coming King—one who would usher in a new kingdom for Israel. During the four hundred years of silence between the close of the Old Testament canon and Jesus' birth, Israel waited in anticipation of the savior who would rescue them from Roman oppression.

The Messiah did come, just not in the way He was expected. Instead of a reigning king or well-trained soldier, He came as the baby of a poor teenage girl. He came as the adopted son of a carpenter, living out His early days in a tiny town by the Sea of Galilee. And when He came into the public eye, He did not rally Israel against their Roman overlords but invited them into a greater kingdom.

Jesus was not the Messiah He was expected to be; He was the Savior the world didn't know they needed.

Jesus, then, was both expected and unexpected. His Jewish family was expectant for the Messiah, but He did not take the form many thought He would. Even today there is some debate about whether prophecies about Jesus were really meant to be about Jesus at all. One answer to this question lies in the *dual fulfillment*, or the "double meaning," of these prophecies.

Think of a word with two meanings. English provides plenty of these; they're called *homonyms*. The word *arm* can mean "the thing attached to your body, holding this book" or "the act of using weapons to defend yourself." Or how about the word *date*? A date can be a fruit, a time on the calendar, or a cute guy who takes you out for coffee. In each instance, the word has meaning but the *context* determines its meaning.

A dual fulfillment prophecy is kind of like a homonym: in its original historical context, the prophecy has fulfillment and application. But it also has fulfillment in a future, Messianic context. Prophecies about Jesus typically had both types of fulfillment.

Dr. David Jeremiah describes the prophecies and psalms about Jesus as "double reference prophecy."[3] This type of prophecy has three distinct characteristics:

- The first fulfillment is found in a person or event close to when the prophet spoke for God.
- This first fulfillment is *partial*; it has more to come.
- The ultimate fulfillment is found in Christ.[4]

So when we look at the promises about Jesus, we're often looking at statements or prophecies that applied *both* to the time they were written *and* to Jesus' birth, life, death, and resurrection. Here are a few:

- The Messiah would be called a Nazarene (Isaiah 11:1; Matthew 2:23).
- He would speak in parables (Psalm 78:2–4; Matthew 13:10–15).
- He would be called a King (Zechariah 9:9; Matthew 27:37).
- He would be betrayed for thirty pieces of silver, and a potter's field would be bought with the money (Zechariah 11:12–13; Luke 22:47–48; Matthew 27:9–10).
- He would be silent when accused (Isaiah 53:7; Mark 15:4–5).
- He would be killed with criminals (Isaiah 53:12; Matthew 27:38).
- He would be a sacrifice for sin (Isaiah 53; Romans 5:6–8).

This is just the tip of the iceberg. Scholars have concluded that Jesus fulfilled anywhere from 300 to 570 Old Testament prophecies.[5] Many of these are woven into the fabric of psalms of worship. Others are part of more immediate prophecies regarding coming judgment on evil nations. Both Jesus and His disciples attributed these prophecies to Christ.

In other words, Jesus is who He says He is—the Son of God.

Proceeding from the Father: The Origin of Jesus

Occasionally when my husband runs errands, he'll text me: "Do you want a latte?" The answer is always: "Do you even need to ask?" It can be safely assumed that, if you are passing a drive-thru coffee place, I will take a decaf coconut-milk latte with a dash of caramel syrup.

Josh assumes I need a coffee, and Christians assume Jesus always existed. It's just a given. We ask no questions. But concern over Jesus' origin was a big deal in the early church! Where, and what, was Jesus before the incarnation (His birth through the virgin Mary)? This question has to do with Jesus' *preexistence*, which means that Jesus existed in reality before He entered our world through the incarnation.[6] Jesus was *up there* before He was *down here*. But what exactly does that mean, and how does it impact us?

INCARNATION: *when the eternal God put on a human nature, body, and person called Jesus, the Greek name for Hebrew Joshua*

The preexistence of Jesus is an important doctrine. If Jesus did not exist with God before He was born of Mary, He would not be equal with God; He would be a *creation* of God (think Greek mythology demigod vibes). This would undermine Jesus' statements of His own deity and equality with God (John 5:17–19; John 14:8–11).

But the most immediate consequence

of believing Jesus did not exist with God before becoming human has to do with God's love. As scholar Douglas McCready wrote, "The doctrine [of preexistence] . . . means Jesus finds His identity on the side of God *before* He finds it as a human . . . [and] explains why the incarnation is an expression of God's love for fallen humanity."[7]

This may sound very distant and irrelevant to your actual life, but stay with me! There are at least two major religions that believe Jesus was not God but a lower-level, "little-g" god created by the Father. You may have encountered people who believe this—right on your doorstep: the Jehovah's Witnesses and the Church of Jesus Christ of Latter-Day Saints (Mormons).

The fact that Jesus didn't just come to earth as "a" god but as God in human form, is a distinctly Christian teaching. And this teaching—God dwelling with humans and giving Himself up for reconciliation—is foundational to the Christian ethic of love.

Early church father Athanasius of Alexandria fought for this doctrine in his famous work *On the Incarnation*. Even in the fourth century, there was a group of people arguing that Jesus was not actually God but just *appeared* to be God (these people were called *Arians*, after Arius, who was a rival of Athanasius). Athanasius wrote extensively to refute this doctrine and was exiled because of it—multiple times! Even when he was kicked out of his own city, Athanasius continued to fight for the truth of Jesus' identity, like he did in *On the Incarnation*:

> You know how it is when some great king enters a large city and dwells in one of its houses; because of his dwelling in that single house, the whole city is honored, and enemies and robbers cease to molest it. Even so is it with the King of all; He has come into our country and dwelt in one body amidst the many, and in consequence the designs of the enemy against mankind have been foiled and the corruption of death, which formerly held them in

its power, has simply ceased to be. For the human race would have perished utterly had not the Lord and Savior of all the Son of God, come among us to put an end to death.[8]

In John 17:5, Jesus Himself affirmed that He existed before the foundation of the world: "Father, glorify me in your presence with the glory I had with you *before the world began*" (emphasis added). Because Jesus existed with God before He existed on earth, He is the expression of God's love in human form.

The Son of Man: The Humanity of Jesus

When I was nine months pregnant with our first child, my husband accepted a job in another state. We debated whether it would be wise to move before or after the baby was born and decided that moving before the birth would be easier than moving with a newborn. At thirty-seven weeks pregnant we moved from Virginia to Pennsylvania. The weeks leading up to that time were scary; none of the hospitals or birth centers would take me so late in pregnancy, something I had not expected. We were finally accepted by a home-birth midwife, which was not our original plan, and only five days after moving, Adeline was born.

That experience was formative for me in many ways, but mostly it gave me a deep reverence for the risk Mary took when she said yes to God. When Mary accepted the call to bear the Messiah, she was accepting a role in an unknown journey—but her faith was in a known and loving God.

God, too, took an incredible risk by sending Himself—His very divine essence and Person—in the form of a human baby. This baby would grow up on earth to experience its burdens and pains and temptations all with one purpose: to live a sinless human life and atone for the sins of the world.

When Jesus came as the child of Mary, He came in the body of a Jewish, male child, complete with all the facets of human nature and its limitations. He did this without surrendering His God-ness. By taking on a human form, Jesus became what Paul called "the last Adam" (1 Corinthians 15:45), a perfect representative to reverse what Adam had done. Jesus is an example of perfectly holy humanity, but He is more than that: He is the God who became King.

Over the course of history people have debated just *how* Jesus took on flesh. Did He deny His divinity to become a baby? Was He actually human, with all the temptations and weaknesses, or did He only appear to be?

The church holds that Jesus' incarnation (becoming God in flesh) requires full divinity and full humanity. This doctrine is so important it was cemented in the Apostles' Creed, a statement of faith established during the first few centuries of the church. The first half outlines Jesus' character, origin, and physical life:

> *I believe in God, the Father almighty,*
> > *creator of Heaven and earth.*
> > *I believe in Jesus Christ, His only Son, our Lord,*
> > *who was conceived by the Holy Spirit,*
> > *born of the Virgin Mary,*
> > *suffered under Pontius Pilate,*
> > *was crucified, died, and was buried.*[9]

The creed was written to outline the fundamental beliefs of Christianity, specifically regarding Jesus' physical body. Remember the Arians, the people who denied that Jesus was fully God? They believed Jesus was a creation of God, like a better, more improved human. There was yet another heretical group called the *Docetists*, and they believed Jesus was fully divine but not fully human. They argued that Christ was born without participating in matter and that His life, ministry, and miracles, including the crucifixion, were not reality but "mere appearances."[10]

Because of these two threats to Jesus' identity, the Apostles' Creed (and eventually the more thorough Nicene Creed) was developed. This statement of faith clarified the Christian beliefs held by the early church, beliefs that were based on and taken from the New Testament. Christians affirm that "the One who had his being eternally within the unity of the Godhead became man at a point in time, without relinquishing his oneness with God. And by the word 'flesh,' he does not mean a physical body only but a complete human personality."[11]

Multiple passages in the New Testament speak to this truth:

- "The Word became flesh and dwelt among us, and we have seen his glory, glory as of the only Son from the Father, full of grace and truth" (John 1:14 ESV).
- "Jesus increased in wisdom and in stature and in favor with God and man" (Luke 2:52 ESV).
- "Since therefore the children share in flesh and blood, he himself likewise partook of the same things, that through death he might destroy the one who has the power of death, that is, the devil" (Hebrews 2:14 ESV).
- "We do not have a high priest who is unable to sympathize with our weaknesses, but one who in every respect has been tempted as we are, yet without sin" (Hebrews 4:15 ESV).
- "Great indeed, we confess, is the mystery of godliness: He was manifested in the flesh, vindicated by the Spirit, seen by angels, proclaimed among the nations, believed on in the world, taken up in glory" (1 Timothy 3:16 ESV).
- "In him the whole fullness of deity dwells bodily" (Colossians 2:9 ESV).

Jesus coming in bodily form is important not just because it's what He claimed and what the church believed. The doctrine of the incarnation, though mystical and mysterious, has an impact on daily life. Here are just a few ways this doctrine affects us today:

- Jesus has fully experienced the suffering of humanity and therefore is the perfect "high priest" to intercede for us in our suffering.
- The fact that God came in physical form is evidence that He values and honors human bodies. He does not consider the spiritual more important than the physical (the belief that physical matter is evil or "bad" is from the religion of gnosticism, not Christianity).
- Because Jesus came as God in a physical body, He is a perfect, sinless substitute for us and our sin, reconciling us to God.
- Jesus' physical resurrection (which we will discuss in a moment) is the foundation of Christian hope and the template for the resurrection of believers after death.

Jesus poured all of Himself, all of His divine power and majesty, into the helplessness of a human child. That child grew up into a man "who, though he was in the form of God, did not count equality with God a thing to be grasped, but emptied himself, by taking the form of a servant" (Philippians 2:6–7 ESV). This does not mean Jesus gave up His divinity to enter a human body but that He assumed the role of humble servant for the entire world. This willing, humble heart paved the way for us to dwell with God. What grace!

To fully grasp the humanity of Jesus, we also have to talk about His divinity. The incarnation of Christ was not just about His human form. It was the majesty of God manifested in flesh. How do we understand Jesus as God?

The Son of God: The Deity of Jesus

Snow fell softly outside, and I watched it twirl in white pirouettes on the sidewalk. I munched on a breakfast burrito in a local grocery café as two men, clad in wool jackets, bent over their cups of steaming coffee a few tables down. I didn't mean to eavesdrop, but their conversation drew me in. It started with a debate about the origins of America, moved to a discussion of a book about the founding fathers, and quickly morphed to a theological commentary on whether Jesus believed He was God.

"He never claimed to even *be* God," sneered one of the men. "It's a misnomer spread by His disciples."

"Interesting," the other man nodded, stirring his drink.

"You'd never know that, though, the way Christians talk about it! The whole church is built on the idea Jesus claimed to be God. If that isn't true, the whole thing falls apart. Can you imagine?"

I *could* imagine. Much rides on the question, Did Jesus believe He was God? If Jesus didn't believe and teach this, if the apostles made it up to create a "new religion," as some skeptics say, the entire foundation of Christianity is, as the men in the café said, lost.

Skeptics of Jesus' deity argue that the Gospels do not say Jesus is God. And in a sense, they are right; Jesus did not state His deity in a manner that English-speaking, Western minds would recognize. But He *did* make a claim to be God—several of them, in fact.

In Mark and John, Jesus frequently engaged with the Jewish leaders in debates over Old Testament doctrine. Jesus quoted titles and phrases about God (taken from Old Testament Messianic prophecies) in reference to Himself—which enraged the Jewish leaders.

Jesus' intentional use of God's name in reference to Himself was appropriate to His Jewish context and audience. Because Jesus came into the world as the Jewish Messiah, it follows that He would use Jewish references to express His divine identity. Unless we engage with the cultural and historical context of Jesus' words, we can draw conclusions about Him that simply aren't true—like believing He never claimed to be God.

One of the boldest statements Jesus made about Himself illustrates this point. To understand it, we have to go all the way back to Exodus 3. Moses, who at the time was a humble shepherd in the wilderness of Midian, had a miraculous meeting with God in a burning bush. God told Moses He would rescue Israel from Egyptian slavery. Moses was concerned the Israelites wouldn't believe Him and asked God to identify Himself:

> Moses said to God, "Suppose I go to the Israelites and say to them, 'The God of your fathers has sent me to you,' and they ask me, 'What is his name?' Then what shall I tell them?" God said to Moses, "I AM WHO I AM. This is what you are to say to the Israelites: 'I AM has sent me to you.'" (Exodus 3:13–14)

This name for God became a foundational truth of Judaism, one marked by great honor and reverence. The name of God was treated with incredible respect.

Fast forward to Jesus in John 8:

> Jesus replied, "If I glorify myself, my glory means nothing. My Father, whom you claim as your God, is the one who glorifies me. Though you do not know him, I know him. If I said I did not, I would be a liar like you, but I do know him and obey his word. Your father Abraham rejoiced at the thought of seeing my day; he saw it and was glad."
>
> "You are not yet fifty years old," they said to him, "and you have seen Abraham!"
>
> "Very truly I tell you," Jesus answered, "before Abraham was born, I am!" At this, they picked up stones to stone him,

but Jesus hid himself, slipping away from the temple grounds.
(vv. 54–59)

Do you see what Jesus was saying? He was claiming the title of
God *for Himself.* This was not the first time He had done this. Jesus
also frequently used the title "Son of Man" (mostly in the gospel of
Mark) as a reference to a prophecy in Daniel 7:

> And behold, One like the Son of Man,
> Coming with the clouds of heaven!
> He came to the Ancient of Days,
> And they brought Him near before Him.
> Then to Him was given dominion and glory and a
>   kingdom,
> That all peoples, nations, and languages should serve
>   Him.
> His dominion is an everlasting dominion,
> Which shall not pass away,
> And His kingdom the one
> Which shall not be destroyed. (vv. 13–14 NKJV)

These were undeniable claims to divinity. Though we're separated from Jesus' culture and time by thousands of years,
understanding the context of His engagement with the Jewish
leaders reveals what He believed about Himself (and what He
expected us to believe about Him). Apologist J. Warner Wallace
put it this way:

When Jesus took on God's holy title as his own, He was stating
the modern equivalent of "I am God." He did this repeatedly
over the course of his ministry (see Mark 14:62, John 18:5–6,
John 8:24 and John 8:28). So while you may not find the expression "I am God" in the Gospels, you'll certainly find the ancient

equivalent. It's no wonder that the Jewish religious leadership would eventually want Him executed.[12]

And that's exactly what happened. The incarnate God was too offensive for the people He came to save—and they sentenced Him to death.

Old Rugged Cross: The Death of Jesus

How do you describe the death of Jesus? When reading the Bible as literature, the crucifixion is the climax of the story. The cross is a recognized symbol of Christ's sacrifice around the world. The death of Jesus on the cross pinned our sin and shame with His outstretched arms. It became an altar of sacrifice unlike any before.

Jesus' death accomplished what the Old Testament saints hoped for and what the New Testament saints relied on: a way to dwell with God. If Jesus is God's love made manifest, the cross illustrates just how far God's love will go. Salvation is "a revelation of the loving heart of the triune God. The Father, moved with compassion, determined from all eternity to send His only Son into the world to redeem men."[13]

What Jesus did on the cross is called the *atonement*. While there are varied theories about how the atonement works, the centerpiece of Christ's atoning work is the love of the Father. There's a tendency in Western Christianity to think of Father God as judgmental or harsh and Jesus as the kinder, more loving "version" of Him. This could not be further from the truth.

Scholar Leon Morris said that "salvation comes to us with all the majesty of God the Father behind it. It is a divine work in the fullest sense."[14] The Father's initiation, His willingness to send the Son as the very expression of His heart in human form, undergirds the entire story of the cross. "The atonement takes place," said

Morris, "because God the Father loves us and makes provision in His Son for our salvation."[15]

This provision was not child abuse. God did not send His Son against His will; Jesus was a willing participant in the entire plan (John 10:11, 15, 17–18). He not only knew the cross could happen, He predicted that it would (Mark 8:31; Matthew 17:22–23; Luke 18:31–34). The love of God the Father was made real at the greatest of costs when Jesus willingly laid down His life to reconcile humanity's sin.

Tears spring to my eyes as I retell the story. What kind of God would go to such lengths to win back His people? The cross we so often take for granted was a weapon of Roman torture. Jesus knew exactly what would happen if He continued to open the kingdom of God to the poor, the weak, and the needy, and He chose to walk the road to the crucifixion. Jesus said, "Greater love has no one than this: to lay down one's life for one's friends" (John 15:13). And this is what Jesus, the ultimate Friend, did for us.

In a world of Etsy cross necklaces and crucifixes in the family room, we tend to forget the significance of Jesus' sacrifice. What exactly happened at the cross? What did the atonement do? Theologians have debated the details of this for centuries, but there are several principles the church generally affirms: the death of Jesus was sacrificial, substitutionary, redemptive, and victorious.[16]

Sacrificial

All of the theories on atonement the church has held—from the first century to present day—affirm that Jesus went to the cross of His own volition. Jesus believed this to be an act of sacrifice (John 3:16; Mark 10:45).

According to the Gospel of John, Jesus died on the Day of Preparation for Passover, just as the lambs were being prepared for sacrifice. The day Jesus was tried, sentenced, and crucified was the same day Israel remembered the exodus. Many years before, the

Israelite slaves had painted their doorways with blood to be "passed over" by the Destroyer in Egypt (Exodus 12). As the Jews prepared to remember this day of deliverance, Jesus was being tried, whipped, and sent to die. Jesus' blood was painted on a wooden beam so judgment and death could "pass over" us. He was, as Christians say at Easter, the Passover Lamb. He was the perfect, purifying sacrifice for sin.

The Old Testament sacrifices acted as "rites of purification" for Israel. God was literally dwelling with them in a tent—the tabernacle—and for this to be possible, there had to be purity. If you're going to live with God, the dwelling must be worthy of Him. The concentrated glory of God rested with Israel and gave them the honor and responsibility of acting as a light to the nations. The sacrificial system purified members of the community and called them to holy lives.

Jesus fulfilled this system. His death was the ultimate act of purification. Because of Him, we are clean (John 15:3). Jesus' disciples, writing about His death on the cross, did not require the sacrifices either. Paul, Peter, James, and John did not reinstate sacrifices for sin because the atonement was enough: "Christ fulfilled [the sacrifices] by His death on the cross. And Paul does not re-institute the death penalty for sins like adultery and homosexuality. Christ took these sins and their penalty on Himself while He was on the cross."[17]

Because of Jesus' sacrificial death, we are vindicated. We are slaves set free.

Substitutionary

One of the most popular atonement theories today, particularly in Reformed denominations, is called *penal substitutionary atonement*. This simply means that Jesus bore a penalty when He died. His death was also "substitutionary" because the penalty He bore was on behalf of others.

This view of the atonement flows from the idea of Adam as humanity's representative, imparting original sin to anyone in his family line (as discussed in chapter 3). This view builds on the idea of the cross as an altar of sacrifice. We assume there must be payment for sin (Romans 6:23) and that Jesus is the sacrificial substitute for us, making a payment we could not afford. Through Christ, God reconciles humanity to Himself.

Not all Christians affirm this view of the atonement. Some believe that God's actions through the cross were not about making or taking a payment but about overcoming the powers of evil. While this may sound the same, the biggest difference is the nature of sin and how God chooses to deal with it. In the *Christus Victor* model of atonement, "God offered life, or reconciliation, and thereby dealt with the effects of sin, such as alienation and death. There is no transaction that disposes God to be gracious so that humankind may be saved; in God's gracious initiative, salvation takes the form of giving life to the world."[18]

In other words, God didn't need a payment to save humanity from individual sins but saved them instead from the *power* of sin through an act of victorious love.[19] With this view, Christ's death was not a stand-in for a penalty but the triumphant ring of victory in the war against evil. Those who give their allegiance to the victorious King become "citizens" of His kingdom: "He has rescued us from the power of darkness and transferred us into the kingdom of his beloved Son, in whom we have redemption, the forgiveness of sins" (Colossians 1:13–14 NRSV). Jesus' substitution of Himself for humanity redeemed them from captivity to sin.

Redemptive

Christians on all sides of the atonement debate agree that Christ's atonement is an act of redemption, as Colossians 1 states. When we speak of redemption, "the idea of a 'ransom' comes into view. A ransom is the price paid to redeem someone from bondage or captivity," wrote scholar Wayne Grudem.[20]

Jesus Himself said, "Just as the Son of Man came not to be served but to serve, and to give his life as a ransom for many" (Matthew 20:28 ESV).

Scholars debate who is on the receiving end of this ransom—the powers of evil or almighty God? With the Christus Victor view, Christ's sacrifice redeemed us from the power of evil. With the penal substitutionary view, we were redeemed from the penalty of sin incurred by Adam. We could even say that we are redeemed from Satan's power because "the whole world is under the control of the evil one" (1 John 5:19).[21]

In either case the end result is peace with God; He has transferred us from one identity to another (Colossians 1:13). We are no longer a part of the old regime. We are part of a new kingdom, a new city, and a new life! We have been brought out of bondage and set entirely free.

Victorious

Jesus' death on the cross is *victory*. "And having disarmed the powers and authorities, he made a public spectacle of them, triumphing over them by the cross" (Colossians 2:15). He defeated His spiritual and physical enemies.

Have you ever wondered why God used Israel to illustrate His love for the world? The story of Israel is an epic tale of God's desire to dwell with humanity and reveal Himself in real time. Jesus was the climax of the story of God and Israel, who was meant to be the light to the nations (Isaiah 49:6). "The point is that the story of Israel was to be a story of how God was going to deal with evil," wrote scholar N.T. Wright. "He would draw it onto one place, allowing it to do its worst at that point. And he himself . . . would go to that place, would become Israel-in-person, in order that evil might do its worst to him and so spend its force once and for all."[22]

Evil did its worst. Jesus took the whip, the cross, the nails, the death, the separation. What seemed like a victory for evil, though, was the opposite! The willing death of Jesus, the innocent, perfect King, was a victory for good.

The Resurrection of Jesus

Have you ever thought about the Easter story? Like *really* thought about it? People around the world gather to commemorate a man, who also happened to be God, *rising from the dead*. The more familiar we are with the story, the less it shocks us, but perhaps we need a little shocking! The resurrection of Jesus is a wild claim. It should come as no surprise that skeptics doubt the validity of the resurrection.

If it is true, it changes the story of history. And if it is not, it ruins the church.

Because skepticism is a cultural norm, we need to know why the resurrection matters. How does Jesus' resurrected body impact us today? Is the resurrection really essential to our faith? The apostle Paul thought so. He took the resurrection so seriously he said that without it "our preaching is in vain and your faith is in vain" (1 Corinthians 15:14 ESV).

He isn't alone! Scholars throughout church history have affirmed the importance of the resurrection. "Christianity is a religion of miracle," said theologian Alan Richardson, "and the miracle of Christ's resurrection is the living centre and object of Christian faith."[23] Though the cross decorates our churches, the power of the gospel is the empty tomb. Without Christ's resurrection our faith is empty, and we are still in our sins (1 Corinthians 15:17). This doctrine is not an extra piece in the gospel story. As Richardson declared, it is the "living centre" of God's redemption of humanity.

The book of Acts shows us how the early church viewed Jesus' miraculous return. Peter talked extensively about the resurrection in Acts 2, his sermon at Pentecost. "God has raised this Jesus to life, and we are all witnesses of it. Exalted to the right hand of God, he has received from the Father the promised Holy Spirit and has poured out what you now see and hear" (vv. 32–33). Not long afterward, the early church leaders were arrested "because the apostles were teaching the people, proclaiming in Jesus the resurrection of the dead" (Acts 4:2). Again in Acts 5, the apostles defended the resurrection to the Jewish religious leaders, saying, "The God of our ancestors raised Jesus from the dead—whom you killed by hanging him on a cross" (v. 30).

If the apostles and early church would fight for such a doctrine, we should be asking ourselves: Why does this matter so much? What did Jesus' resurrection practically accomplish?

Scholar Ralph Earle provides one answer to this question: "The resurrection of Jesus proved that his sacrifice for sins had been accepted. The whole redemptive scheme would have fallen apart without it."[24] If we consider how the apostles treated the resurrection, this theory makes a lot of sense. The disciples of Jesus believed His claims to be God, but the resurrection *confirmed* it. They were witnesses to a miracle—a miracle that changed their lives.

Gary Habermas, the leading scholar on the resurrection, was on staff at my alma mater when I was there studying religion. When he wasn't coaching hockey (he's a Michigander like me!), he wrote and taught extensively on the historical proofs for the resurrection of Jesus. In an article he wrote shortly after losing his wife to cancer, Habermas stated that the resurrection of Jesus is the first and primary hope for Christians facing suffering. The proofs of the resurrection provide a framework, real history, to which we can anchor our faith.[25]

This answers our question, Why does the resurrection matter so much? It matters because Jesus' triumph on the cross finished the work of our salvation. His death atoned for it. His rising proved that sin and death have no power over the life-giving God, no power over Jesus, and no power over us. Though we will still die on this earth, our lives in Christ begin *now*. This is why Paul could cry out to the Corinthian church, "Where, O death, is your sting?" (1 Corinthians 15:55). Because of Christ's victory, we go from life to life.

Easter Sunday is a day to celebrate the bold, wild, unstoppable God who defeated the sting of death. It's a day to remember the immovable faith of believers who, for centuries, have trusted the historical testimony of hundreds of eyewitnesses. Easter reminds us that resurrection isn't just for Jesus; it's also for us. One day we, too, will "rise again" to join Him in glory. "For if we have been united with him in a death like his," Paul wrote to the Roman church, "we will certainly also be united with him in a resurrection like his" (Romans 6:5).

HOW WERE PEOPLE IN THE OLD TESTAMENT "SAVED"?

When reading the Gospels, we inevitably wonder how people came to salvation before Christ. Were the Old Testament saints left high and dry without a Savior to redeem? After all, they didn't know the name of Jesus. How could they believe and be saved?

Both Jesus and the apostles spoke about this issue multiple times. In Romans, the apostle Paul pointed to Genesis 15:6: "Abram believed the LORD, and he credited it to him as righteousness." This, he said, is evidence that the Old Testament believers were saved by faith just like those under the new covenant in Christ.

Peter said a similar thing about the prophets. They "searched intently" into "the time and circumstances to which the Spirit of Christ in them was pointing when he predicted the sufferings of the Messiah and the glories that would follow" (1 Peter 1:10-11). The prophets saw

God's promise in the words they spoke for the Lord, and their faith in God saved them.

Lastly, Jesus used the Old Testament to show His listeners how He fulfilled God's promises. In Luke 24, Jesus said, "Everything must be fulfilled that is written about me in the Law of Moses, the Prophets and the Psalms" (v. 44). Jesus went on to explain how the law, prophets, and writings—the three primary sections of Scripture in the Jewish Bible—point to His Person. These were the Scriptures available to the Old Testament saints, whose faith in God's promised Messiah was counted to them as righteousness.

Chapter 5

Soteriology: No Longer a Slave

THE DOCTRINE OF SALVATION

There was no escaping. The whir of red and blue, the shrill scream behind me. My anxious eyes glanced at the dashboard—too late. It was too late.

Only a few weeks after moving to Virginia, I was stopped by a police officer between Appomattox and Lynchburg on my way to work, caught in the sneaky bait-and-switch of a speed trap. Perhaps it wasn't so sneaky; I was flying through the forty-five-mile-per-hour zone at a breakneck seventy. The officer waited for people like me, college girls in cheap red cars. He pulled me over, wrote me a ticket, and told me I could appeal in court to have the significant points on my license taken off.

I'd never been in court before. The pretty brick building gleamed in the April sun, innocently peering between dogwood blooms. *The only innocent thing present,* I thought. Clicking through the hall in my work heels, I slipped into the back of the court. Finally, they called my name, and I took my place before the judge and the officer who had pulled me over. All I felt were eyes—the eyes of the others in court, the eyes of the officer, the eyes of the judge—boring holes into me, the one who always had to rush, the one who was always late.

Others had told me what to expect and what to do: "When you go in, they'll call your name. The judge will ask the officer what happened when he pulled you over. He'll ask you how you plead. You'll say guilty." I'd agreed to all of it, willing to do anything to keep the points off my license. So there I stood, prim in my work skirt, staring up at the judge.

"How do you plead?" he asked.

"Guilty."

Guilty. It's a difficult word to acknowledge. You're probably a better driver than I am and have a lot fewer speeding tickets (it's not hard to do). I hope you've never had to show up in court for reckless driving. It's not fun. However, the experience of standing before a judge granted me a new perspective on the biblical analogies to civil law in the first century. The Bible frequently uses legal language to describe our salvation and the process by which Jesus bridged the gap between us and God. The Bible's teaching on salvation is described theologically as *soteriology.* Scripture uses legal language—guilt, payment, freedom, and judgment—to tell us what salvation does. Legal terminology is used in First and Second Timothy, Galatians, First and Second Corinthians, and Romans to describe how the gap between us and God is closed. God is a judge. Through Christ, we are justified before God.

SOTERIOLOGY: *the study of Christian salvation from sin*

When we see legal language in the New Testament, we often imagine a criminal act like my speeding. But Paul may have been speaking to a different legal situation: the freeing of a slave. *Manumissio vindicta* was a simple Roman ceremony Paul was undoubtedly familiar with (he referenced similar themes in First Corinthians). In *vindicta*, the master and slave would appear before a Roman official accompanied by a Roman citizen. The Roman citizen would touch the slave's head with a staff and declare him free. The master, who until now was holding the slave, turned the slave around and let him go with the words "*hunc hominem liberum volo,*" meaning, "I want this man to be free."[1]

The fall of humanity in Genesis 3 enslaved humanity to evil. Ever since evil was chosen by Adam, we've experienced the pain of a fallen world. We've been separated from God's perfection, unable to dwell with Him the way He intended. As discussed in our last chapter on Christology, Jesus' life, death, and resurrection were God's "rescue plan." Like the slave before the Roman judge, we stand captive to evil, longing for freedom. And like the advocate, the Roman citizen, Jesus stands with staff in hand to appeal for that freedom and release us. To be saved is to be set free!

Soteriology contains three vital elements: justification (a change of identity from sinner to saint), sanctification (the process by which we become like Jesus), and glorification (the final result of Christian life). Christian thought is incredibly diverse, offering multiple perspectives on each of these elements. Salvation theology combines what we've learned about the nature of Scripture, God, the universe, and sin to explain God's ultimate goal: restoring people to Himself.

In the next few pages we will explore:

- how Christ's atonement grants us a change of identity;
- how the cross frees us from sin eternally and presently;
- how we can walk out our new identity with increasing holiness; and
- our hope for future glory.

Justified By Faith

The book of Romans—Paul's great theological treatise—discusses the process of justification at length, but he sums it up succinctly in chapter 4: "To the one who does not work but trusts God who justifies the ungodly, their faith is credited as righteousness" (v. 5).

It's clear from this verse and its context that Jesus' atoning sacrifice saves us not by any work of our own; our lack of perfection prevents us from reaching God on our own strength. Our faith in Christ, our "shift in allegiance," as scholar Matthew Bates put it,[2] grants us a righteousness we could not earn with all the good deeds in the world.

In other words, we don't work for salvation; we trust for it.

Some Christians believe God chooses ahead of time who will trust in Him by regenerating their hearts and enabling them to respond. Others believe God sovereignly grants His people the ability to respond to His initiative of their own accord. Either way, this trust results in righteousness, and that process is called *justification*.

But what does justification mean, exactly? I love how nineteenth-century Anglican bishop Handley Moule described it. To be justified, he said, is more than being forgiven by God. It means "being received by Him as if we had not grieved Him."[3]

Christ is the catalyst to a complete identity transformation. Jesus' death on the cross was effectual for all who put their faith in Him. The grace imparted through faith removes our past life and identity. God takes us into His arms as children, as if we had never broken His heart through sin. The righteousness of Christ completely absorbs who we were before we met Him!

This transformative experience of God's justice is not just a release from bondage. As Moule went on to say, we need more than forgiveness. We need more than an escape route from sin. We need "the voice which says, not merely, 'You may go; you are let off your penalty'; but, 'You may come; you are welcomed into My presence and fellowship.'"[4] Justification is both the clang of freedom's bell and a shout of "welcome home!"

The atoning sacrifice of Christ gives a final verdict: those in Christ are part of a new family, released from sin and gathered to God's arms. Paul described this power in his letter to young pastor Titus:

> But when the kindness and love of God our Savior appeared, he saved us, not because of righteous things we had done, but because of his mercy. He saved us through the washing of rebirth and renewal by the Holy Spirit, whom he poured out on us generously through Jesus Christ our Savior, so that, having been justified by his grace, we might become heirs having the hope of eternal life. (Titus 3:4–7)

Salvation, Paul wrote, is not something we receive because we're good enough or wise enough or fast enough or flashy enough. Righteousness is by faith and grace, and through the justification of God we receive eternal life. Here Paul employed another strong image: that of an heir to a great inheritance.

I'm a bit of a period-drama guru. I eat up those Masterpiece classics like *North and South*, *Mansfield Park*, and *Little Dorrit*. In so many of these movies, and the books upon which they are based, the future of a main character depends on an inheritance. If you don't get an inheritance, you need to marry someone who does. If you do the wrong thing, you can be disinherited. How many times is a female character passed over for the girl with a bigger inheritance? Too many!

In these dramas, and in Paul's day, an inheritance was protected with certain laws and regulations to make sure the correct person received the estate. Sometimes it required a coming of age.

Other times it was dependent upon their career choice. If the person fulfilled the requirements of the "law," they could receive their inheritance.

Not so with God! The inheritance we did not deserve and could never earn became ours through Christ. It's as if He, the true Heir, drapes His royal robes over our shoulders and says, "She is one of mine. She is a coheir." The Greek word *dikaloo* means "to declare righteous," and this is exactly what Christ does for us.[5] All the rewards of perfect righteousness—peace with God, insurmountable joy, security in God's love, reconciliation, forgiveness of sin—are accessible to us through our new identity as heirs in Christ.

Let's skip back to the Roman ceremony of *manumissio vindicta*. Can you picture it? The master holds the slave, a staff touches the bowed head, and there come the words of liberty: *I want you to be free*. With one turn around, the slave is a free man. Keep this image in your mind as you read Paul's words to the Galatian church:

> In the same way we also, when we were children, were enslaved to the elementary principles of the world. But when the fullness of time had come, God sent forth his Son, born of woman, born under the law, to redeem those who were under the law, so that we might receive adoption as sons. And because you are sons, God has sent the Spirit of his Son into our hearts, crying, "Abba! Father!" So you are no longer a slave, but a son, and if a son, then an heir through God. (Galatians 4:3–7 ESV)

We are left to conclude what the apostles affirmed: to be a Christian is to embrace a new identity. We are completely forgiven, granted a rich inheritance, and invited into Edenic fellowship with God. We've been changed—and this changes everything.

Branches of Salvation Theology

Reimagine your faith-family tree: strong and ancient with a rising trunk and branches reaching to the sky. I can almost hear the birds gathering in the branches, singing the praises of God and the people who knew Him. Your Christian family tree is rich with history.

But your Christian family tree involves more than you and more than your family; it includes the entirety of the church—every believer from past, present, and future. As you may have noticed, many of those believers belong to different types of churches than you—what are sometimes called *denominations*. How should we understand these groups and subgroups within the church?

Think of Christianity itself as the trunk. Each denomination (which just means "out of the name"), a subgroup within Christianity, is a branch on that tree. These groups did not develop because of petty fights over the church carpet or debates about hymns. Most denominations were born because of theological differences over important doctrines like salvation.

The creeds sum up Christian fundamentals—the trunk of our family tree. The branches are formed when intelligent Christians ask, "How?"

How does baptism work?
How did God save His people?
How does the Holy Spirit grant spiritual gifts?

All Christians agree that salvation, baptism, and the Holy Spirit are essentials of our faith. But we differ on *how* those essentials function. When it comes to salvation, people have theorized about its process for the entire two thousand years of church history. These debates never threatened the trunk of the tree; they just grew more branches. And as long as Christians unite around the core truths, our "branches" can intertwine and mingle peacefully.

Sadly, many Christians do not expose themselves to the other branches. They don't read material outside of their denominational comfort zone. And because they don't understand how the other branches arrive at their biblical conclusions, they fight. They argue. They condescend. They lose their love.

We can change this. By understanding the soteriological perspectives of other Christians, we equip ourselves to have productive conversations and even better relationships! Following are four perspectives on salvation from your brothers and sisters in the faith, the people walking with you on this road to Christ. These are not specific denominations. They are *views* of how salvation works, and they may be found in any number of denominations around the world (with the exception of Roman Catholicism, whose theology and church are bound together as one).

By including these, I am not endorsing every single teaching of these denominational groups. Rather I am encouraging you to begin a lifelong journey of understanding what other Christians believe.

Roman Catholic

The Roman Catholic Church has a long Christian history. Catholics believe their first pope, the father of the church, was Peter (Matthew 16:18). Upon his death a succession of popes acted as bishop of Rome and continue to do so today.

Roman Catholics view salvation as initiated by God. God is the one who draws us to repentance, an act of grace toward sinful humans. What happened at the cross was a "deposit of grace," to use the inheritance analogy again. Humans may receive this grace or reject it; grace does not restrain the human will.[6] This is distinctive, however: the sacraments of the church are used by the Holy Spirit to continue dispensing that "deposit of grace" into the lives of believers. The indwelling Holy Spirit resides in every Catholic, the Church teaches, but the sacraments are a vital, material way to experience God's gracious salvation.

Human participation in salvation is important. The convert's partnership with God in salvation by "work[ing] out [her] salvation" (Philippians 2:12) makes it effectual. Justification is not just a declaration of righteousness but an actual transformation, making the disciple just in God's eyes.[7] This is walked out in sanctification, which is becoming more like Christ. Perhaps one of the most distinctive elements of Catholic theology is the unity of justification and sanctification: God's salvation must be worked out and *will* be worked out by those who are truly saved.

Unlike the Protestant salvation theologies, Catholics don't have a neat acronym summing up their position. Much ink has been spilled to outline their position, however, especially following the Protestant Reformation. The Council of Trent of 1545 clarified the teachings of the Catholic Church, including their stance on salvation.

Eastern Christianity

Eastern Christian tradition is often forgotten in American discussions of theology, which is ironic because Christianity began in the Middle East! Eastern Christianity has four main branches: the Eastern Orthodox Church (which is headed by the Patriarch in Constantinople/Istanbul), the Oriental Orthodox, Assyrian Church of the East, and Eastern Catholic. The Catholic churches are headed by the pope, though there may be some differences in practice. The Patriarch of Eastern Orthodoxy is believed to hold the office of the apostle Mark, much like the pope in Rome is believed to hold the office of Peter.

When Christianity began, Rome was an important government center. After the fall of the Roman Empire, the church's role was vital in the rebuilding and consequential development of civilization in the West. The Roman Catholic Church was the Latin-speaking branch of the Christian world; the Eastern Orthodox Church spoke Greek. But these were not the only differences between the two. Though they worked in tandem for a thousand years, the Great Schism of 1054 separated the Roman Catholic and Eastern Orthodox churches for good. They continue to operate as separate entities today.

Salvation theology in Eastern Christianity is similar to Catholicism in respect to the relationship of faith and works. Eastern churches affirm original sin; we cannot do a spiritual good that will save us from judgment. But this sin did not destroy human ability to choose God's salvation through Christ. Humans must cooperate with God in His salvation, and good works are the outworking of true faith: "We regard works not as witnesses certifying our calling, but as being fruits in themselves, through which faith becomes efficacious."[8]

In Eastern tradition, God's salvation is available to all who respond to His initiating grace. God desires for all people to be saved (1 Timothy 2:4) and knew who would respond to Him before the world was created. Those who He knew would respond, He elected to be saved. Orthodox churches hold to an idea of *prevenient* ("come before") grace similar to what we see in Wesleyan-Arminian traditions—meaning that God gives a kind of grace by preparing our hearts to respond to Him in faith.

One distinctive practice of Eastern Christianity is the use of icons during worship. Icons are elaborate paintings, or pictures, of Christ, Mary, and saints of the church. Eastern Christians use icons as a reminder of the incarnation. Just as Jesus, our spiritual God, took on a material body and form, the material form of icons reminds believers of the spiritual truths they represent.

Calvinistic Reformed

The early church laid a foundation for the truths of Jesus' life, the hope of salvation. The creeds and councils cemented those truths. But like ivy entwines around a foundation, damaging it in time, theology unchecked can go in ungodly directions. That is what happened to the church. The Latin-speaking church in Rome began to teach ideas beyond what the Bible said about faith and good works. Some of their priests and scholars spoke out about it. This clash of theology resulted in what is now known as the Protestant Reformation, which eventually resulted in the development of a salvation theology often called Calvinistic Reformed.

Though the words "Calvinist" and "Reformed" are often used interchangeably, these two words mean slightly different things. A Calvinist adheres to principles of faith systemized by John Calvin, a famous Reformer of the church. Calvin, along with Martin Luther (who attempted to reform the Catholic Church but ended up breaking from it), wrote prolifically on theology. The Reformers were a group of Christians who formed churches outside of Catholic oversight. Today most, if not all, Reformed churches are Calvinistic, but not everyone who is Calvinist is Reformed.

Reformed theology can usually be summed up with three Cs: Calvinistic (as represented in the acronym TULIP), covenantal, and confessional.[9]

Calvin's theological work sought to describe salvation through faith and grace alone. After experiencing spiritual abuses by the Roman Catholic Church of the time, Protestants sought a return to a more biblical narrative of salvation based on faith and grace. Calvin's *Institutes of the Christian Religion* summarized these concepts and many more. Later on, his views were condensed into the acronym TULIP:

- **T—TOTAL DEPRAVITY:** Better described as total inability, the *T* in TULIP represents humanity's complete inability to reach or respond to God. Because humanity is "dead in sin," Calvin and other Reformers believed they could not respond to God at all, even if He offered them salvation.
- **U—UNCONDITIONAL ELECTION:** Election is the process of choosing someone for salvation. Because humanity can't

respond to God, His election is "unconditional," or unaffected by human response. God chooses who will be saved based on His sovereign will. Before He even made the world, He predestined them to be saved.

- **L—LIMITED ATONEMENT:** The atonement of Christ on the cross applied only to those who God elected (chose) to be saved (Ephesians 1).

- **I—IRRESISTIBLE GRACE:** Because God's Word cannot return void, those who God elects and atones for will inevitably embrace His grace. God's grace in salvation cannot be resisted or rejected.

- **P—PERSEVERANCE OF THE SAINTS** (often called "once saved, always saved"): Because God has elected, atoned for, and saved those He has chosen, they will remain in their salvation unto the end. Those who reject salvation after professing faith in Christ were never saved in the first place.

This is an extremely short summary that does not do justice to the range of work Calvin and other Reformers provided. However, TULIP is important because it is distinctive to Calvinistic thought and the Reformed view of salvation.

Reformed theology is also covenantal as it sees the biblical narrative through a lens of God's major covenants. These are summarized differently depending on the theologian you read, but generally speaking the covenants are redemption, works, and grace. The covenant of redemption was God's plan for the world from the beginning (Isaiah 53:10–12; Psalm 2). The covenant of works was offered to Adam in Eden; if he obeyed, he would have peace with God. Adam broke this covenant, and God mobilized the covenant of grace: the promise of Jesus Christ (Genesis 3:15).

Reformed theology is also confessional, though this could be said of all the Christian traditions. To be confessional means there are certain realities or truths about God, Jesus, the Spirit, Scripture, and the Christian life that must be believed in order to call oneself a Christian. Reformed theology confesses doctrines beyond those basics that align with their specific view of salvation.

Calvinistic Reformed theology can be found in Dutch Reformed, Reformed Baptist, Presbyterian, Lutheran, Christian Reformed, and nondenominational churches around the world.

Wesleyan-Arminian and Anabaptist

Around the same time Calvin and Luther were doing their work, another Reformer named Jacobus Arminius was teaching at the university of Leiden in Amsterdam. Arminius initially agreed with John Calvin's view of predestination: God chose ahead of time who Jesus would save and who He would not. But as he continued to study, Arminius changed his mind. He believed this view of God's sovereignty sacrificed His mercy and did not align with the character of God in Scripture.

Arminius presented a different view of salvation: whoever responds in faith to God's love in Christ is considered "elected" for salvation.[10] Humans cannot earn their salvation or reach God of their own accord, but salvation is open to all who, by faith, lay hold of God's loving initiative.

Later followers of Arminius, called Remonstrants, outlined their own principles in response to Calvinistic theology in the Articles of Remonstrance (1610). Like Calvinism's TULIP, Arminian theology can be summed up in an acronym as well: FACTS.

- **F—FREED BY GRACE TO BELIEVE:** God, in His sovereignty, freed His creation to respond to His salvation or reject it. God used His free will to create free will in humanity.
- **A—ATONEMENT FOR ALL:** God desires all people to be saved (John 3:16) and His atonement is available for anyone who calls on the name of the Lord. Only those who respond to that salvation offer will be saved.

- **C—CONDITIONAL ELECTION:** God decided to save (elect) only those who put their faith in Christ. While there are different views on election among Arminians, most believe that God elects to salvation those who respond to His offer—whom He knew would respond before they were born. His sovereign knowledge does not mean He caused them to choose Him but that by giving them free will and pursuing them in Christ, He offered them the option.

- **T—TOTAL DEPRAVITY:** All humans are separated from God by sin and cannot save themselves. This depravity keeps us from peace with God but does not remove the image of God in us. God must initiate salvation.

- **S—SECURITY IN CHRIST:** Jesus secures our salvation and the Holy Spirit empowers us to remain in Him. Most Wesleyan-Arminians do not believe you can "lose" salvation but that, if you reject it, you either were never saved or are willfully walking away from faith.

Around the same time as Arminius, another Christian group called the Anabaptists (which literally means "rebaptizers") was born. This group was not directly affiliated with the Reformers, Calvinists, or Arminians, but their salvation theology more closely aligns with the Arminian stance than it does Calvin's.[11]

Meanwhile, in England, a group called the Separatists (having separated from the Church of England) began meeting privately to worship. Similar to the Anabaptists in Germany and the Netherlands, this group believed in believer's baptism after a profession of faith rather than the infant baptism practiced in Catholic and Anglican churches. Persecuted for their faith, the "Baptists," as they were now called, spread throughout England and then to America. Though some Baptists held to more Calvinistic or Puritanical views, others held a salvation theology more aligned with Arminius.

A few centuries after the Reformation, Anglican pastor John Wesley built upon the work of Jacobus Arminius. Wesley's prolific writing on total depravity, the freedom of human will, and God's saving grace was so extensive that we now call Arminian theology Wesleyan-Arminianism. Wesley founded small Bible studies for men and women to teach them the fundamentals of faith and practice. These studies eventually became the Methodist Church.

Over time, the Wesleyan-Arminian and Baptist theological tradition expanded across the Atlantic and then around the globe. (It was, and is, the most missions-focused theological tradition.) Descended from the Wesleyan-Arminian family tree we find the Methodist, Nazarene, Wesleyan, Holiness, and charismatic/ Pentecostal churches, as well as some nondenominational churches. The Anabaptist tradition continues today in the Mennonite, Amish, and Brethren communities, and the Baptists are represented by many different denominations bearing their name.

The range of Christian thought on salvation is wide and beautiful, like a tapestry hung on the wall. The threads weave in and out, different colors each offering their part to a masterpiece: *God with us. Emmanuel.*

However, it is hard to remember—when we focus on the individual threads—that understanding does not equal agreement. We may never fully agree with another branch on the Christian tree. We might even find other viewpoints problematic. But if these brothers and sisters affirm the fundamentals of faith (Acts 15) and are growing in holiness (Galatians 5), we can walk together with them as the image of Christ on earth. We become the *body* of Christ.

This unity is vital to the church. Christianity is not a religion of isolation; it is a faith community, a place of being, a place to know and be known. As we align our theology with Scripture and graciously walk with fellow believers, we become more and more like Jesus. And isn't that the point?

Imaging God on Earth: Sanctification

Black coffee steamed and curled from the demitasse cup on the table my father had built. We were all gathered for Dad's birthday. The farmhouse beat to the rhythm of toddler feet and sibling laughter as we gathered for the cake Mom had made. Outside the snow drifted in from the west, the way it does in March.

"What person, other than your parents or spouse, shaped you most?" Mom read the question from a Table Topics card and, before anyone could speak, quickly added, "Can't be Jesus!" My siblings chuckled, then paused as every heart searched its history: *What person shaped me most?*

When it was my turn, I knew the answer. "I have two," I replied, picturing faces from years ago. "Dr. Cliff Kelly and Ken Winter." Both men were professors. One taught me to wield a pen, the other to use my voice. Their roles in my life were academic, but they were more than teachers to me.

"Okay, why?" Mom asked.

I thought for a moment. "Both of them believed in me. They continually told me I was a writer—a good writer—and that I would go far if I kept at my craft. They spoke success over me before it ever existed." I paused. "I would have followed them anywhere."

When someone bends to embrace what they know you could be before you're even there, it's a particular kind of grace. It's a grace pulling upward, drawing you to your feet, filling your lungs with air. It's a grace that says: *I know what you can be. Trust me.*

Was there a teacher, an aunt, or a woman at church who spoke this to you? Powerful words follow us like goodness and mercy.

The goodness and mercy of Dr. Kelly and Ken follow me now; I hear their voices, their guidance, each time I finish a paragraph or page. "Don't wrap up the story so tightly," Ken says over my shoulder, pointing to the screen. "You don't need it. The rest of the work speaks for itself." They spoke an identity over me: *You are a writer. You will find your way. You can go further.* They gave me something to live up to.

If salvation is an identity change, we, too, have been given something to live up to. We've been given an entirely new frame of reference for life. Sanctification is just a fancy word for "becoming more like Jesus." To the degree we live up to our righteous identity, we are sanctified (purified) into the image of Christ. My professors spoke an identity over me that shaped my gifts and future career. Christ speaks—and secures—an eternal identity for us that shapes our souls and future lives in Him. Growing up in that salvation, that identity, is *sanctification.*

> **SANCTIFICATION:**
> *the living out of our holy identity, progressively becoming more like Jesus*

Paul continued to use the analogy of slave versus freedman in his letters to Galatia and Rome. "For freedom Christ has set us free; stand firm therefore, and do not submit again to a yoke of slavery" (Galatians 5:1 ESV). *You were turned around and liberated!* Paul was saying. *Don't go back to who you were before.*

The world perceives Christians as moral rule followers. It's the old, "Don't smoke, drink, or chew, or go with boys who do" kind of morality—follow the rules. Do the right thing. Keep up appearances.

But the moral standard of Christianity is not about following rules. We already know we can't earn salvation or close the gap between ourselves and God. Anything we do *after* salvation can't be for that purpose, either. So why do Christians live holy lives? The answer lies in Galatians 5:1: "For freedom Christ has set us free."

Christ didn't set us free from slavery so we could memorize a list of behaviors. He set us free so we could experience an entirely new identity, a new *reality*. We choose holiness, purity, and sanctity not because we have to but because we *want to*. Jesus has spoken a new identity over us. Holy isn't something we do. It's who we are. It's what we live up to.

This identity is not earned on our own strength, but we must exert spiritual strength to walk in it. This is why Jesus gave us the Holy Spirit (John 14:15–31). The Spirit of God empowers us to choose actions aligned with our Christian identity. We reject gossip, rage, hatred, drunkenness, and sexual promiscuity (Galatians 5:19–21) not because we're afraid of God, but because we've experienced the richness of His love and the beauty of life in Him:

> You are a chosen people, a royal priesthood, a holy nation, God's special possession, that you may declare the praises of him who called you out of darkness into his wonderful light. Once you were not a people, but now you are the people of God; once you had not received mercy, but now you have received mercy. (1 Peter 2:9–10)

Did you catch that? You, church, are chosen, royal, holy, special. And because of this, you declare the praises of the One who set you free.

Identity precedes action.

We see it again in Colossians 1:

> We continually ask God to fill you with the knowledge of his will through all the wisdom and understanding that the Spirit gives, so that you may live a life worthy of the Lord and please him in every way: bearing fruit in every good work, growing in the

knowledge of God, being strengthened with all power according to his glorious might so that you may have great endurance and patience, and giving joyful thanks to the Father, who has qualified you to share in the inheritance of his holy people in the kingdom of light. For he has rescued us from the dominion of darkness and brought us into the kingdom of the Son he loves, in whom we have redemption, the forgiveness of sins. (vv. 9–14)

Paul reminded the Colossian church of their mission—to bear fruit, to do good works, to grow in knowledge and power—but he did so in context of their *identity*. It is useless to pursue these "Christian behaviors" apart from the identity of someone who has been freed. To do so will result in either legalism or burnout or both.

The only sustainable way to live the Christian life is by the Spirit's strength. The holiness of the Christian life brings us full circle: back to the image of God in the garden, the broken and incomplete image so far from God's first intent. Through Christ, the broken image becomes whole. The incomplete "idol" of God on earth becomes a complete picture of Christ-in-us.

Jesus takes the throbbing heart of humanity, the little spark of God's goodness struggling against sin, and fans it into flame. Fire purifies. Fire warms. Fire shows the way. No wonder the Holy Spirit comes by fire—His presence makes lights of us (Acts 2). We are meant to *ite, inflammate omnia* (a phrase attributed to church father Ignatius)—to "go, [and] set the world on fire."[12]

Glorification: The End Game

Even if this world were set aflame for the gospel, it would still be an imperfect and feeble house for the Lord. The two things God cursed after the fall were the Accuser and the ground. These cursed

entities would impact Adam and Eve, and
the men and women they represent, for the
entirety of life on earth. Both Adam and
Eve labored to bring forth life (he from
the ground, she from her body). Those of
us who are in Christ still experience the
heaviness of a broken world. Sanctification grows us into the image
of Christ, but this process cannot end here on earth. There must
be more.

GLORIFICATION:
*the final removal of sin
from God's people*

Glorification is the final state of Christian salvation, the end
game of God's justifying, sanctifying love. Glorification is when sin
and sickness are fully removed, when we are completely freed of
them. "Now we see only a reflection as in a mirror; then we shall
see face to face," wrote Paul. "Now I know in part; then I shall
know fully, even as I am fully known" (1 Corinthians 13:12).

Fully known. This, really, is the heart of the gospel: to be fully
known by God. This God reached down to an unreachable people,
grasped them in His almighty hand, and offered them a chance to
dwell with Him. In this age, the dwelling is still marred with sin. We
are broken-down houses. In the next age, the glory of God in Christ
will be fully revealed and we will no longer be imperfect dwellings
for a perfect God. When He makes all things new, our old bodies,
lives, and struggles will be absorbed in His glory.

Moses had to veil his face after beholding the glory of God, and
he couldn't even look directly at Him (Exodus 34:35). But we will
behold Him with unveiled face (2 Corinthians 3:13) as we are transformed into the very image of our Savior. The body of Christ—the
church—will one day be united to the King. His glory will be our
glory. His peace, our peace. We will be in a constant community
of sisters and brothers, dwelling in God's presence without death,
sorrow, crying, or pain (Revelation 21:4–5).

Salvation's eternity begins now. We hope for future glory, but we
experience the power of Christ today. We get to live into a righteous

identity and walk with the indwelling God. What God is so great that He would limit Himself to a human body and willingly suffer and die just to bring His people back home? We cry with the psalmist: "Who is this King of glory? The LORD strong and mighty" (Psalm 24:8). Because God reached down through Christ, we are the embraced, the chosen, the loved—and as we accept this reality, we "proclaim the excellencies of him who called [us] out of darkness into his marvelous light" (1 Peter 2:9 ESV).

The Light is coming. The Light is here. Those who have seen it can't help but proclaim it. We've been taken from the darkness, from the separation, from the sin. We've been adopted, inherited, exalted—all because Christ laid Himself down. We've seen the Light, and not just seen it—we carry it in our hands and hearts: a little flame of grace.

And with such a flame, we set the world on fire.

SEPARATION OF CHURCH AND STATE

The Arminians and Anabaptists were heavily persecuted by the Calvinist Reformers, just as the Calvinists had been persecuted by the Catholics, and just as the Catholics were eventually persecuted in the "New World" of America. At times in history, theology had a direct impact on one's community and even one's safety. Because theology was interwoven with kingdoms and governments, it even led to war.

As the years went by, the persecution of Baptists, Puritans, Methodists, and Catholics led many of these groups to immigrate across the sea to the New World. Here they hoped to live in peace. Freedom of religion was so important to these groups that their situation was kept in mind during the writing of the United States of America's founding documents. In a letter to the Danbury Baptists, a group of Christians who feared persecution, US president Thomas

Jefferson promised a "wall of separation . . . between church and state"[13] to protect them from the persecution of a state-endorsed church. In the United States today, denominations may disagree on doctrine, but they are not limited from worship by a governing church body.

Chapter 6

Pneumatology: Like Flames and Doves

THE DOCTRINE OF THE HOLY SPIRIT

I stacked them high on the little secretary desk: books. On the desk, the floor, in baskets. I wanted to know all I could. I had to move the stacks off the desk to have room for writing or my elbow hung off and the cursive drooped. Slips of paper, old letters, ribbons, pens—jammed in every small pocket of the desk—spilled onto the books as I took notes. At sixteen, I was new to Jesus and eager to learn *everything*.

I'd hung beads in my bedroom doorway. I liked how they looked. They reminded me of hippies, though I wasn't supposed to be one. I was at my desk staring at the beads, chewing an eraser, when Dad came in. He leaned a callused hand against the doorway and parted the beads with a tolerant smile. "Like the seventies, eh?" He chuckled. I smiled, turned my journal over. He glanced down.

"What's this?" He turned over the top book. *The Perfect Christian.*

"I found it on the shelf, probably from Grandma's stuff," I said hastily. Dad was kind, but I felt foolish. I wanted to know it all, to do it right.

"You know," Dad said, setting the book back down, "you don't have to try that hard."

I rolled my eyes. "We can't all be perfect like you, Dad."

"I'm not perfect, you know that. I'm saying: these books aren't what helps you be a Christian. They aren't what makes you a follower of God."

I crossed my arms. "Then what does?"

A simple version of the answer to that question is just three words: *the Holy Spirit.* When we go deeper into the expanded version of that answer, it's called *pneumatology,* or the theology of the Holy Spirit. (*Pneumatology* comes from the Greek *pneuma,* which means "spirit" or "wind.") This "ology" sums up everything the Bible says about the Spirit's helping, advocating, empowering, purifying nature.

PNEUMATOLOGY: *the study of the Holy Spirit*

I Will Send You a Helper

After Jesus rose from the dead, the Gospels and the book of Acts tell us He spent forty days with His disciples before ascending to the Father. In those days He proved His bodily resurrection, but He also continued teaching the disciples and told them what to do when He was gone:

> After his suffering, he presented himself to them and gave many convincing proofs that he was alive. He appeared to them over a period of forty days and spoke about the kingdom of God. On one occasion, while he was eating with them, he gave them this

command: "Do not leave Jerusalem, but wait for the gift my Father promised, which you have heard me speak about. For John baptized with water, but in a few days you will be baptized with the Holy Spirit." (Acts 1:3–5)

This was not the first time Jesus spoke of the Holy Spirit. He prophesied the Spirit's coming earlier in the Gospels:

If you love me, keep my commands. And I will ask the Father, and he will give you another advocate to help you and be with you forever—the Spirit of truth. The world cannot accept him, because it neither sees him nor knows him. But you know him, for he lives with you and will be in you. I will not leave you as orphans; I will come to you. (John 14:15–18)

Other translations say "helper" instead of "advocate." This Helper, the very Spirit of Christ remaining with the disciples, would equip them for the task ahead: building the church. The disciples were understandably concerned about Jesus' departure. Acts 1 describes them looking up to the sky in bewilderment when Jesus ascended. I can imagine them wondering, *What now?* And then they remembered Jesus' command: *Wait for the gift.*

The Holy Spirit was not new to the disciples. They were familiar with Him from the Old Testament accounts. But in Torah, He takes a slightly different role. Under the old covenant God gave to Israel through the law, the Holy Spirit "came upon" prophets, priests, judges, and kings to equip them for specific tasks. The Holy Spirit equipped for leadership (Numbers 27:18), wisdom (1 Samuel 16:12–13), and artistry (Exodus 31:2–5). In addition, the presence of the Spirit could be lost by repeated sin (such as in the case of Saul in 1 Samuel 16:14).

The Spirit Jesus promised was no different from the Spirit of the old covenant. He provided the same equipping and presence.

The difference after Jesus is His *permanence*. The Holy Spirit is our Helper, not just for one task or temporary calling but for all of life in Christ. Jesus knew we could not live the new life on personal power. He wanted His disciples to make full use of His presence—and He wants us to do the same.

The Holy Spirit in Scripture

Dad picked up the book on my desk and flipped idly through the pages, ignoring my crossed arms. "Your desire to do the right things is good, Phy," he said. "But being a Christian is not about white-knuckling good deeds or being 'the perfect Christian,' as this book promises."

"Well, what else am I supposed to do? How else am I supposed to do what's godly? It certainly doesn't *feel* easy, if you say it isn't so 'hard.'" I didn't even try to hide my irritation. Honestly, the Christian life didn't feel easy or light to me—it felt like one long haul of trying to obey.

"It *is* hard," Dad replied. "I'm not denying that. But the difficulty isn't in doing good things. That's not where your energy is to be directed. You're to focus on letting the Spirit guide you. Follow His voice. Rely on His leading, which will never contradict the Bible. It's not about memorizing lists of what to do or not do. He will *tell* you what to do." He turned and parted my hippie-bead doorway, the pink cascade of beads a wild irony against his builder's plaid shirt.

"You have a Helper," he said. "Let Him help."

You might relate to my teenage struggle. Perhaps faith does feel heavy to you. Perhaps you are memorizing the fruit of the Spirit and trying to do them on your own strength. Maybe you're like sixteen-year-old Phylicia, sitting in the parking lot of my summer job at the greenhouse, pink Bible in one hand and sandwich in the other.

I had memorized the passages about Christian behavior: love, joy, peace, purity, honor, respect. I would rehearse them, hop out of my cheap red convertible, and muscle my way through the workday on willpower-morality.

I suppose this is what Dad foresaw that day by my desk: the force of white-knuckle Christianity—driving hard, giving it all, right before the crash and burn.

Let Him help. Don't do it alone.

That's always been the Spirit's role: to help. To advocate. To empower. From creation, when He hovered over the waters in union with Father and Son, three Persons in one holy God, the Spirit's presence poured out goodness. He empowered beauty, order, and peace, and He still does in the world and in us. He helps us become like Christ. Without Him sanctification isn't possible. But when forming a theology of the Spirit, we must look to Scripture as our guide.

It gives us some clear patterns by which we can understand the Spirit. Here are a few:

- He is one with God at creation (Genesis 1:1–2).
- He is the giver of life (Job 33:4).
- He gives wisdom and understanding (Isaiah 11:2).
- He is grieved by sin (Isaiah 63:10).
- He instructs in righteousness (Nehemiah 9:20).
- He gives us a new heart (Ezekiel 36:26–27).
- He is the Spirit of truth and conviction (John 14:15–17).
- He dwells with believers after repentance and baptism (Acts 2:38).
- He gives power (Romans 15:13).
- He dwells in believers (1 Corinthians 3:16–17).
- He reveals God's love to us (Romans 5:5).
- He bears the fruit of good works (Galatians 5:22–23).

If it seems like the whole Christian life is dependent upon the Spirit's work . . . that's because it is! In the Old Testament, God dwelt among His people in temples made by hands. Today, He dwells in human bodies. The "idols of God" on earth are little sanctuaries of His grace. And as the Holy Spirit lives in us, He is at work—empowering us to live in the light, guiding us into good works, and bringing fruit into the world through us.

The Person of the Holy Spirit

Many Christians forget the power of being Spirit-holding image bearers, temples of the Most High God. When we don't learn a biblical pneumatology, we lack motivation to be holy; it's completely out of reach. If we don't know the power of the Holy Spirit, we won't walk by His leading. And if we don't walk by His leading, our lives won't bear fruit.

To walk with someone, you must trust them. We usually don't hold hands with strangers. Likewise, to walk by the Spirit—to listen to Him and let Him lead us—we must know His voice and trust it. We must be willing to unite ourselves to His purpose. We must know Him for the Person He is.

The rise of New Age spirituality makes the personhood of the Spirit very important. The New Age movement uses terms that sound like biblical spirituality but mean something very different. The New Age does not require one specific set of beliefs but teaches that truth is individual, encouraging followers to seek "deeper wisdom," connect with spirits, and commune with nature. Because the New Age is rising in popularity, we must be clear on who the Spirit is and what He is not.

The Spirit of Christ is a real person—not a force, not a vague entity, not a "spirit in the sky" uniting us to the universe. He is the expression of Christ on earth through God's people, the church. We know the Holy Spirit is a person by His relationship with the Father and Son (John 16:14–15; 2 Corinthians 13:14). Jesus attested to His coming, promised His presence, and told His disciples to wait for Him (Matthew 28:19).

The Spirit also portrays personal characteristics such as emotion (Ephesians 4:30), wisdom (Isaiah 11:2), and intercession (Acts 20:23). The character He cultivates in people reflects His nature. The Spirit's work is opposed to the world's patterns:

> The acts of the flesh are obvious: sexual immorality, impurity and debauchery; idolatry and witchcraft; hatred, discord, jealousy, fits of rage, selfish ambition, dissensions, factions and envy; drunkenness, orgies, and the like. I warn you, as I did before, that those who live like this will not inherit the kingdom of God. But the fruit of the Spirit is love, joy, peace, forbearance, kindness, goodness, faithfulness, gentleness and self-control. Against such things there is no law. (Galatians 5:19–23)

We can know something is "of the Spirit" if it bears His fruit! Because He is love, He cultivates love. Because He is joy, He brings about joy. Because He is peace, He brings us peace.

Like any person, the Holy Spirit has a name—actually, more than one! The names of the Spirit give us hints regarding His role in our lives and in the world:

- He is the Dove at Jesus' baptism, descending from the Father (Matthew 3:16).
- He is the Advocate, sent to teach us the things of God (John 14:26).
- He is the Spirit of Jesus, continuing Christ's presence with us after His ascension (Acts 16:6–7).

- He is the Intercessor, praying for us when we have no words (Romans 8:26).
- He is the Lord (2 Corinthians 3:17).

The Deity of the Holy Spirit

"I think Jesus rides on the back of the Holy Spirit," my brother Anders announced at the dinner table when he was six years old. He went on to admit that he didn't know what the Holy Spirit was. A ghost? An angel? He was trying to work it all out. While we may not imagine such a distinctive visual, many of us are in a similar position—we don't know what we think about the Holy Spirit!

In addition to being a Person, the Spirit is equal and eternal with God. While maintaining oneness with God, He holds a distinct role: sustaining and bringing life to God's creation.[1] Some commentators on Genesis believe the breath with which God raised Adam to life was the Spirit Himself (Genesis 2:7).

The Holy Spirit shares God's attributes. He is omnipresent (in all places, Psalm 139:7–8), omniscient (all-knowing, Isaiah 40:13), and omnipotent (all-powerful, Zechariah 4:6; Luke 1:35). He is eternal (Hebrews 9:14). Throughout the Bible the Spirit is identified with God and His authority, being sent by God and promised by Jesus. In the Old Testament, He is called "the Spirit of God" or "the Spirit of the Lord."

Perhaps the boldest testament to the divinity of the Spirit is the fact it's possible to blaspheme Him (to curse Him in word or lifestyle): "Anyone who speaks a word against the Son of Man will be forgiven, but anyone who speaks against the Holy Spirit will not be forgiven, either in this age or in the age to come" (Matthew 12:32).

This blasphemy has been defined as an "ongoing hardening of the heart" against the Holy Spirit's leading, conviction, and call to repentance.[2] It is a continual resistance to the loving call of God's heart. Because the Spirit is the "bringer of life," resisting Him is to resist God Himself and invite the opposite of life—death and separation.

The Ministry of the Holy Spirit

Let Him help. Dad's words hung in the air. Sixteen-year-old me was frustrated and confused by anything other than bootstrap Christianity. *Jesus saved me, and now I work it out . . . right?* The fruit of the Spirit were committed to my memory, trained in my mind one day at a time. Yes, I felt tired at times. Sometimes I resented God for it, but isn't that part of the journey? I told myself it was.

Dad's kibosh on my "perfect Christian" endeavor frustrated my young heart. I did not know or understand the ministry of the Spirit. I did not have a framework for the freedom He offers—no idea how open, wild, and good the walk with God can be.

I understood Christianity in terms of following rules. But the Spirit whispers something much different: *This is adventure.*

As a person of the Trinity, the Spirit works in both the unbelieving people of the world and the followers of Christ within the church. His ministry differs in these places.

In the world, the Spirit seeks to convict people of their sin and draw them to life in Christ:

> I tell you the truth: it is to your advantage that I go away, for if I do not go away, the Helper will not come to you. But if I go, I will send him to you. And when he comes, he will convict the world concerning sin and righteousness and judgment: concerning sin, because they do not believe in me; concerning righteousness, because I go to the Father, and you will see me no

longer; concerning judgment, because the ruler of this world is judged. (John 16:7–11 esv)

Jesus explains the Spirit's ministry to the world as a trifold ministry of conviction, righteousness, and judgment. As vessels of the Spirit, followers of Christ participate in this ministry. The Spirit uses Scripture, creation, conscience, and the lives of Christians to convict the world of sin and show them the way to righteousness.

Our role as temples of God's Spirit should never be underestimated! God is at work in the world, and we get to be part of it.

The Spirit also ministers to, in, and through the church. The church is simply the collective gathering of Spirit-filled believers in Christ. The church is not a building; it is *people*. Because we need the Spirit to draw us to Jesus and work salvation in our lives, you could say the church is "founded" by the Spirit! In this worldwide gathering of renewed hearts, the Spirit continues His ministry by equipping church members with specific gifts. These gifts differ from person to person, and together the Spirit of God uses them to bless the world.

The Gifts of the Holy Spirit

In the fifteen years between teenage Phylicia and today, I became a wife and mom to three. On my thirty-first birthday, there was a gentle knock on the door. A little face, eyes large and eager, peered through the crack. When she saw I was awake, a gap-toothed smile crept across her face, and my little girl walked in with an array of treats. "Breakfast in bed for your birthday!" she beamed as her squealing sister followed her. It didn't matter that breakfast was one piece of peanut butter toast and that crumbs undoubtedly filled the kitchen. My four- and six-year-olds had made me breakfast! What a gift.

There is nothing quite like a heartfelt gift. Perhaps I'm a bit biased; gifts are my love language. Nothing brings me more joy than "brown paper packages tied up with string," to quote *The Sound of Music*. But gifts would be boring if everyone were distributed the exact same ones. It's the surprise, the personalization of a gift, that blesses us.

The Spirit personalizes His gifts to the people of God, but He does not do so for their own glory or attention. He gives us gifts so we may bless others, reach the world, and glorify God. These gifts are described a few times in Scripture, specifically in 1 Corinthians 12 and Romans 12.

In 1 Corinthians, the apostle Paul informed his readers that the Spirit distributes these gifts for the upbuilding of the church. The "many parts" of individual believers' lives make up "one body" in Christ, equipped to serve one another and the world:

> There are different kinds of gifts, but the same Spirit distributes them. There are different kinds of service, but the same Lord. There are different kinds of working, but in all of them and in everyone it is the same God at work.
>
> Now to each one the manifestation of the Spirit is given for the common good. To one there is given through the Spirit a message of wisdom, to another a message of knowledge by means of the same Spirit, to another faith by the same Spirit, to another gifts of healing by that one Spirit, to another miraculous powers, to another prophecy, to another distinguishing between spirits, to another speaking in different kinds of tongues, and to still another the interpretation of tongues. All these are the work of one and the same Spirit, and he distributes them to each one, just as he determines. (12:4–11)

In his letter to the Roman Christians, Paul outlined a similar but slightly different list of gifts:

Just as each of us has one body with many members, and these members do not all have the same function, so in Christ we, though many, form one body, and each member belongs to all the others. We have different gifts, according to the grace given to each of us. If your gift is prophesying, then prophesy in accordance with your faith; if it is serving, then serve; if it is teaching, then teach; if it is to encourage, then give encouragement; if it is giving, then give generously; if it is to lead, do it diligently; if it is to show mercy, do it cheerfully. (12:4–8)

Consolidated, the spiritual gifts are:

- discernment
- service
- teaching
- encouragement/words of wisdom
- generosity
- leadership
- faith
- healing
- miracles
- prophecy
- speaking in tongues
- interpretation of tongues
- mercy

These gifts help us serve others the way Christ came to serve us. That's why discovering and using our gifts should not be focused on learning more about ourselves, as if the gifts are just another personality quiz. The Holy Spirit gives us practical strengths for the purpose of service.

My gifts are teaching and discernment. I use these gifts to serve the church by educating people about the Bible, directing them to spiritual disciplines, and discipling them one-on-one. My friend Sarah has a gift of encouragement and mercy. She is full of compassion and quick to build up others with her words. My husband, Josh, has a gift of service, or administration. He is gifted at organizing behind the scenes and executing detailed plans. The church needs all of us!

The goal of Paul's lists was not to systemize gifts into a neat little quiz. Because these traits are gifted by the Spirit of God, the closer we are to Jesus, the better we will understand our spiritual gifts. We'll also be quick to recognize the gifts of the Spirit in others! As the Holy Spirit works in our hearts, we become confident in His equipping. And in daily life with other Christians, our gifts will never *compete* but will always *complement*.

Some of the gifts Paul mentioned may give you pause. Prophecy, healing, miracles, and tongues (the languages spoken spontaneously in Acts 2 and the early church) may sound foreign to your Christian experience. Your understanding of these gifts is likely connected to your church's theological stance on them. *Cessationist* churches believe miraculous gifts have ceased in Christian practice. *Continuationist* churches believe the gifts of healing, prophecy, miracles, and tongues continue today and should be practiced to advance the gospel and edify the church. Let's quickly dive into each of these stances.

Cessationist churches believe, as a general rule, that the foundation laid by the apostles and prophets (Ephesians 2:20) gave the church all it needed for future ministry. The work of the apostles and prophets is recorded in the Gospels, Acts, and the epistles, and this work included prophecy, healing, miracles, and tongues. These gifts were essential for the establishment of the early church but ceased to be necessary after that period of time.

Some cessationists cite Hebrews 1:2, "in these last days [God] has spoken to us by his Son," as evidence that God no longer speaks to His people through miraculous or prophetic means. When the apostles died and the canon of Scripture was compiled, cessationists believe the need for the miraculous gifts also died out.

Continuationist churches argue that the miraculous gifts were not just for the early church period and the apostles; they were for all believers and all time. The biblical evidence for Christians acting in the miraculous gifts is found throughout the book of Acts and in several epistles (Galatians 3; 1 Corinthians 12–14; 1 Thessalonians 5). In 1 Corinthians 13, right after outlining the spiritual gifts, Paul wrote that the spiritual gifts would not pass away (vv. 8–10).

A significant difference between cessationist and continuationist churches lies in a definition of terms. Cessationists believe prophecy and other miraculous gifts are adding "new revelation" to the Bible. For example, if someone has a "word from the Lord," a cessationist is usually skeptical or even resistant, since some believe God only speaks through the Bible, not personally Spirit to spirit. They argue that such revelation (a personal encounter with God) is unnecessary now that the canon is closed.

But continuationists do not believe the miraculous gifts add anything new to Scripture (they shouldn't!) but that the gifts should instead *affirm* existing truths. Continuationists also object to separating out the gifts of tongues, healing, and prophecy while other gifts of service, teaching, and leadership continue today.

In charismatic and Pentecostal (continuationist) church traditions, you'll see the miraculous gifts practiced in varying degrees. Some of these churches make the mistake of seeking "the Spirit" as if He only operates in sensational and exciting ways. When this happens, the practice of miraculous gifts becomes a competition to see who is more "spiritual" or "in tune" with the Holy Spirit. This is not how these gifts are to be used! The Holy Spirit brings beauty, order, and peace wherever He goes. He may also inspire miraculous gifts, but He will do so while reflecting the order of God's creating intent: "The spirits of prophets are subject to the control of prophets. For God is not a God of disorder but of peace—as in all the congregations of the Lord's people" (1 Corinthians 14:32–33).

However, in noncharismatic (cessationist) church traditions, Christians may fail to acknowledge the sovereignty of God's Spirit. When we put Him in a tidy box of our own making, we're attempting to tell God what is and isn't acceptable for His Spirit to do. To be a Christian is to be witness to the miraculous! We must be open to the fact that God's Spirit "blows wherever it pleases. You hear its sound, but you cannot tell where it comes from or where it is going" (John 3:8).

Continuationist churches must remember the Spirit brings order; cessationist churches must not let their order prevent the Spirit's work.

The Fruit of the Holy Spirit

In the last chapter we discussed why Christian morality is not a list of rules. That's what sixteen-year-old Phylicia wanted: a nice, neat checklist. Something I could sign my name on, a way to say, *I'm doing this Christian thing right*. But the way to do the Christian life right is much simpler than that.

Jesus would say it is easy and light (Matthew 11:30). Paul said it this way: "Walk by the Spirit, and you will not gratify the desires of the flesh" (Galatians 5:16). The "flesh" is your pre-Jesus identity. Remember the *manumissio vindicta*, the Roman ceremony where a slave is officially freed? *You* were pronounced free. You are no longer a slave. To act like a slave is to live into your old, unredeemed humanity.

But that is not who you are.

In Christ, we have a new life, new hope, new purpose. But most of all, we have the Spirit of Christ dwelling within us, empowering us to live up to that new identity in Him! Practically speaking this means relying on His leading in each decision of the day. When deciding how to respond to a nasty email: *Lord, how would You have me write this?* When arguing with your spouse: *Lord, how do I respond like You would?*

When my dad objected to *The Perfect Christian* book, I felt attacked. I liked the promise of an impersonal Christian faith. But that was Dad's point: Christianity is intensely personal. The Spirit is dwelling in you, with you, shaping and forming you to look like Jesus. That takes daily interaction with Him! It takes listening for His voice. The Spirit's job is to remind us of all the things Jesus taught us (John 14:26).

Certainly, Bible memorization is an important practice. That's a spiritual discipline. And in the moment of struggle, the Spirit uses that discipline of the past to empower us in the present. When we feel overwhelmed at the prospect of trying to change ourselves into "good Christians," the answer is not pulling ourselves up with more Christian tasks. It's to *let Him help us.* Ask for His leading. Listen for His voice. Obey by His strength.

As a saint in Jesus, you have a responsibility to image Him—to reflect His heart in the world. We all do. But we can't muscle our way into that reality on our own. We have to allow the Spirit to transform us, which involves having ongoing contact with God. The Holy Spirit bears the fruit of the Spirit in our character *to the degree we let Him.* His role is transforming us, and our role is to rest, remain, and live in connection to God through prayer—an ongoing heartfelt conversation—so we know His voice and are ready to obey Him. This is how we are sanctified, or purified, into Christ's image.

We can, however, choose instead to resist the Spirit's sanctifying work in our hearts, and when we do, we grieve Him:

Do not grieve the Holy Spirit of God [but seek to please Him], by whom you were sealed *and* marked [branded as God's own]

for the day of redemption [the final deliverance from the consequences of sin]. (Ephesians 4:30 AMP)

The key to bearing God's fruit and becoming holy, godly image
bearers is to remain in step with the Spirit. To "walk by the Spirit"
means to not take a step forward without remembering Him, listening for Him, and relying on Him. This posture of the heart
is so different from willpower Christianity. It's not striving; it's
attachment.

> You are already clean because of the word I have spoken to you.
> Remain in me, as I also remain in you. No branch can bear fruit
> by itself; it must remain in the vine. Neither can you bear fruit
> unless you remain in me. (John 15:3–4)

Imagine the One who planted the first garden describing how to
bear fruit: *Remain. Let Me help you.* Since the fruit of the Spirit are
given by the Spirit of Christ, we can safely deduct that the fruit Jesus
described in John 15 is the same fruit Paul described in Galatians
5: "love, joy, peace, forbearance, kindness, goodness, faithfulness,
gentleness and self-control" (vv. 22–23). It is worth noting that the
fruit of the Spirit are not like the spiritual gifts—we don't have only
one or two; we are meant to bear them all! And if we want to be
loving, joyful, peaceful, patient, kind Christians, we must remain
attached to the Spirit of Jesus. We must remain in step with His
voice.

This attachment is just what Jesus described in John 15: *Abiding.*
Resting. Remaining with Him. He will never leave nor forsake us,
but how often do we "leave" Him with our thoughts, choices, and
behaviors? And if Jesus expects us to be holy as God is holy (1 Peter
1:16), our attachment to Him is key.

Walking by the Spirit does not guarantee an emotional change.
You may not *feel* like obeying His voice. You may pray and ask

for strength or patience and still not feel it before stepping out in obedience. This is faith! Walking by the Spirit is *faith* that God will supply your every need in Christ Jesus, including your emotional capacity (Philippians 4:19).

The better we know Jesus and His voice, the more passionate about obedience, more aligned with holiness, and more committed to kindness we become. The law tells us what moral behavior is wrong and anti-Christ (Exodus 12; Galatians 5). However, we obey it not by striving but by abiding.

The Spirit does not force Himself upon people. He is a Person, loving and wise, ready to counsel us in the hardest decisions. He is our Comforter, ushering us forward on the days we feel like we can't take one more step. He is the dove, full of peace and purpose. But He is also the flame, burning with power, ready to refine the impurities keeping us from a stronger walk with Christ. He is most of all the Advocate and will do whatever it takes to make us more like God. Without Him, the Christian life is powerless.

As evangelist D.L. Moody put it: "There is no use in attempting to do God's work without God's power. A man working without this unction, a man working without this anointing, a man working without the Holy Ghost upon him, is losing time after all."[3]

WHAT DOES SPIRIT-LED PROPHECY LOOK LIKE TODAY?

The Old Testament is full of prophecy—whole books of it! But Paul also listed prophecy as one of the gifts of the New Testament church. He indicated that prophets may be members of the regular church community, including the female church community (1 Corinthians 12–14). This would be nothing new since women are mentioned as prophets in the Old Testament also (Miriam, Deborah, Huldah, Isaiah's wife).

In continuationist churches prophecy is still practiced, but the intent is not to write new books into the Bible. In both the Old and New

Testaments, prophets were people who spoke to the people of God through the Spirit of God.[4] Prophecy under the new covenant in Christ follows this same pattern with the added requirement that whatever is said lines up with the revealed Word of God (Scripture).

In the Old Testament, prophets relayed visions and messages from God, but they also explained the practical impact of obeying or disobeying God's law. In the new covenant church, people with a gift of prophecy might spontaneously speak a word of conviction by the Spirit's leading, or they might share how the Word of God applies to a specific situation. Thus prophecy today might look like theological teaching, encouragement, or equipping for ministry.[5]

Chapter 7

Ecclesiology: A City on a Hill

THE DOCTRINE OF THE CHURCH

The home I grew up in was built with my father's own hands. He was only twenty-eight years old when he and my mom bought the sandy, fifteen-acre farm where he'd build my mama's dream, where six kids would run happy and wild for the next fourteen years. He built it, and then they continued to build it: changing wallpaper and paint, rearranging rooms, renovating, and remodeling until the day the house sold. They built something so beautiful, every memory I have still lives there.

Dad built the house all at once, but he also built it slowly. In the years that passed, the house became more and more what he originally meant it to be. It never stopped being the thing he had built at the beginning, and yet it became something intrinsically more. For my parents, the house was never "done." It was constantly becoming a better version of what Dad had envisioned.

When the Holy Spirit draws people to Christ, and those people respond, those renewed image bearers become members of a new family, a new household of faith. With Jesus as the cornerstone, those believers are joined together as the church. "Church" is an Old English word descended from the Dutch *kerk*, in turn descended from the Greek *kuriakon*, or "Lord's house."

But, as we've said before, the house in reference is not a building. The house is *the people*.

> You are no longer foreigners and strangers, but fellow citizens with God's people and also members of his household, built on the foundation of the apostles and prophets, with Christ Jesus himself as the chief cornerstone. In him the whole building is joined together and rises to become a holy temple in the Lord. And in him you too are being built together to become a dwelling in which God lives by his Spirit. (Ephesians 2:19–22)

In our last chapter we learned about the power of the Holy Spirit and our great privilege to act as temples of His glory. Our bodies house the Spirit of Christ. We have access to all the goodness of God because of the Advocate! The Spirit's presence is a powerful advantage to us, but His influence isn't simply for our self-improvement. He unites us with other believers.

Christianity was never meant to be a solitary sport. Our faith is inherently communal. That Christianity is a personal pursuit divorced from community with other believers is not a product of Scripture or history; it's a product of individualism. In the United States such "rugged individualism" is admired, applauded; the people who pull themselves up without relying on others are seen as heroes.

Biblical Christianity offers a different way. Instead of independence, Christ offers *interdependence*. As we depend on the Spirit, we unite with other believers, relying on them and ministering alongside them. With Jesus at the center, we are all "built together" as a dwelling for God. People look at us together and see Jesus.

This is upside-down from what many Christians believe about

the Bible. We read it as if it's written to us personally, not to us and fellow Christians. But what if our witness is not only about personal character? What if it is about our personal character *in context of community*? It is much harder to bear the fruits of godliness in relationship than it is when going solo!

I believe this corporate witness is exactly what Jesus was after. It was Jesus who said "You [plural] are the light of the world. A city set on a hill cannot be hidden" (Matthew 5:14 ESV). A city is made up of many people, not just one. Continuing this thought, most of the New Testament is directed not at individuals but at groups. The epistles of Paul, Peter, James, and John were all written to *groups* of Christians. When the apostles say "*you* are no longer foreigners and strangers," the *you* refers to a collective, not to a single person reading the letter alone. These letters would be read publicly to the gathered believers. The use of *you* referred to the church as a whole.

This corporate mentality carried over from the Old Testament. The New Testament word for *church* comes from the Old Testament word *kahal*, which refers to the assembled people of Israel. Faith is communal. To be a Christian is to be part of a community, on both the worldwide and local level.

The book of Acts gives us a vivid picture of early church life. From this account (which can be considered "part two" of Luke's gospel), we learn what the church is, what it should be doing, how it should be structured, and what ministry it offers to its members and the world.

A Definition of "Church"

Ecclesiology, based on the Greek word *ecclesia*, is the theology of the church. As I write this book, the confusion and hurt over church runs like a jagged scar across Christendom. We are confused over what church is. Is church a sermon and worship service and altar call?

Is church a small group Bible study in a living room? Is church hype music and a light show to draw people in? Is church a walk through nature, as some argue it to be?

While the word *ecclesiology* refers to the Greek term for "assembly," the word *church* is taken from the Greek term that means "dedicated to the Lord." The church, then, is a gathering of people dedicated to the Lord. They don't need a specific building, style of music, or service structure to be a church. They must simply affirm the core truths of Christianity as people dedicated to God.

ECCLESIOLOGY: *the theology of the church, its mission, and its structure*

Jesus knew exactly what He was doing when He left His disciples waiting in Jerusalem. Those who say Jesus did not set out to create a new religion misunderstand His own words. Jesus set out to offer the indwelling Spirit (1 Corinthians 3:16) and a gathering of people in His name (Matthew 18:20). Those united in His name (united in His nature[1]) were promised the presence of Christ. They were to live holy lives, lighting the world's way to God.

Jesus *did* create something new. He founded the church.

It was new for the Spirit of God to dwell in believers, empowering them to live out a law written on their hearts (Jeremiah 31:33). But the church was also the continuation of a story that began in Genesis 3. After the fall destroyed God's perfect dwelling place with humanity, God promised a redeemer who would make all things right. Then Adam and Eve's children descended into great corruption. The sin of humanity was so great that God had to judge their violence. In Genesis 9, only one man, Noah, was preserved from God's judgment.

But even after the flood of Genesis 6–8, the people went back to their self-worshiping ways. They built a tower to the sky, a temple to "make a name" for themselves (Genesis 11:4). Instead of filling the earth with image bearers of God, they congregated in one spot and forgot their purpose. God confused their languages, and the tower became known as Babel, the ancient predecessor to Babylon, which represented not just an anti-God culture but an *attitude* of idolatry. It is from this part of the world, this dark, fallen, Eden-upside-down world, that God called a man: Abraham.

Abraham was not special. He was human just like us. But when God told Abraham His plan to use Abraham's family to bless the world, Abraham "believed the LORD, and he credited it to him as righteousness" (Genesis 15:6). Though Abraham and his wife, Sarah, were old, God miraculously provided them a family line, one through which the Messiah would one day come. Abraham's family would be "a light to the nations—so that all the world may be saved" (Isaiah 49:6 GNT).

Do you catch the parallel? Israel was a light to the nations. The church is the light of the world. The church is the *continuation* of God's purpose for Israel. This is why Paul called the church "the Israel of God" (Galatians 6:16).

This confirms what *ecclesia* tells us: Faith is not meant for isolation. Church is by nature an assembly, a united front of faithful Christ followers, a union of temples being built into one greater temple to God. When the apostles used *ecclesia* in the New Testament, they did not mean a building called "church" but "the assembling of saints for worship."[2] The city on the hill is *Christians, corporate.* As we grow together, our individual lights gather into one shining beacon to welcome wanderers home.

The Purpose of the Church

Newly married, Josh and I were a few months into living in a transient city. Few people stayed in our university town for more than the required four years, and making connections was hard. We threw our effort into connecting with others at our church. The only opportunity for service was providing refreshments, so we joined forces with some elderly church members once a month to set up coffee and set out muffins.

After a few shifts I began to wonder: *Is this what the church is supposed to be doing? Is this what I am supposed to be doing in the church? Serving muffins?*

Maybe you've had this moment in the baby nursery. Or on the worship team. Or even in pastoral ministry. Is *this*—all of this American, structured, play-by-play, streamed-service stuff—what the church is supposed to be doing? *Is this it?* We have to look back to Scripture to know.

After Peter's sermon on the rooftop in Acts 2, three thousand people came to know Jesus as Lord. *Three thousand!* While there is no doubt many of these people had been in Jerusalem for the festival and returned home after Pentecost, many others would have stayed and been integrated into the existing Jerusalem church. Acts 2:42 describes the early church meetings: "They devoted themselves to the apostles' teaching and to fellowship, to the breaking of bread and to prayer."

Let's look again at these four components that characterized the beginning church and should characterize our church gatherings today:

- the apostles' teaching
- fellowship with other believers
- breaking bread (sacraments, which some call Eucharist and others call Communion)
- prayer

These four characteristics alone didn't make the early church as powerful as it was. Luke went on to say that a sense of awe fell on every person (Acts 2:43)—a sense of overwhelm, reverence, and amazement at the work of Christ. A church full of people in *awe* of God's goodness can't help but light the world! This new community rejoiced in their forgiveness and the gift of the Holy Spirit.[3] They did not resent gathering or find it inconvenient to learn from the apostles; they were eager to share life in Christ with one another.

Today, we think we must get the perfect programs, music, and aesthetic to keep people "in the church." But the draw for early Christians wasn't what a church building could offer. The draw was Jesus. The opportunity to learn more about Him and how to walk in His Spirit prompted these Christians to gather together in awe of God. Connecting in shared faith, shared mission, and shared burdens with fellow believers—however imperfect—united the church and still should today.

Churches across denominational divides structure their services to incorporate the four elements of teaching, fellowship, sacraments, and prayer. After the apostles died, their teachings were canonized as doctrinal and ethical instructions based on the teachings of Jesus Himself.[4] As believers internalize this Scripture, their lives reflect Christ's transforming Spirit:

> As new members joined the community, they were offered these foundational teachings in order to deepen their understanding of the way of Jesus that they had chosen to follow. The communal life is more than just warm-hearted fellowship among believers. The resurrection has truly transformed the priorities and social arrangements of their former status quo.[5]

Perhaps this is why we are dissatisfied with a "fellowship" of little more than serving muffins. It's not the muffins' fault (who can shame a quality muffin?); we lack a change of priority in the church. When individuals don't reorient their lives around their new family, a new family can't exist. We show up, serve (or eat) muffins, listen to a sermon, and leave. This isn't how any real, lasting community is built. Families deepen relationships by consistent exposure and vulnerability. Clubs unite around a united vision or goal. The church is far more than a club but still requires vision. And the church *is* a spiritual family, but cultivating such deep relationships takes more than consuming a Sunday sermon once a week.

The early Christian experience was transformative. It was united. It was holy. And it was *growing*. Not always in numbers but definitely in maturity. The Holy Spirit inspires holiness and unity in a gathering of believers, and from this unique lifestyle of love, they minister to the world.

The Ministry of the Church

I don't want to make our refreshment service sound like a terrible assignment. It wasn't. But it did leave me asking, *How can I really serve the church and the world in a way that meets true needs?* Some days the "true need" really may be a muffin in the church lobby, but I think we all know there are more dire needs than that. If the church is a gathering of Christ-transformed people, it should be a place of powerful influence and grace. How that grace is poured out to the body of believers and world is the church's *ministry*.

Theologians differ on how many kinds of ministry exist in the church. The ministry of the church is different from individual believers' gifts. This ministry is corporate; it is the end result of all those gifts working together. The primary expressions of church ministry are teaching, fellowship, worship, service, and evangelism.

Teaching

Teaching ministry is one of the most visible ministries of the church. Teaching is the exposition of Scripture, explaining what it means and how to live it out. If the church is a classroom for

Christians, the Bible is the textbook! Teaching ministry is important because it equips believers to know *why* they believe what they believe. As culture becomes increasingly post-Christian, this is essential.

Biblical literacy—the ability to read, understand, and apply Scripture—is lacking in American churches despite access to every kind of Christian material imaginable. Although churches cannot force people to learn, they are tasked with the responsibility to provide sound teaching to their assembly.

This responsibility is a heavy one. Teachers are shaping the Christian view of God and the world. James warned teachers that they would be judged with greater strictness (James 3:1–3). Because teachers are in more visible and authoritative positions in church, they can become enamored with their own influence and power. This prideful end can be avoided when teachers recognize their calling: to serve and equip.

As Paul said, "Christ himself gave the apostles, the prophets, the evangelists, the pastors and teachers, to equip his people for works of service, so that the body of Christ may be built up until we all reach unity in the faith and in the knowledge of the Son of God and become mature, attaining to the whole measure of the fullness of Christ" (Ephesians 4:11–13).

The goal of teaching ministry is to build up the church into unity, knowledge, and maturity. If a teaching ministry centers on the teacher, it is no longer achieving its biblical end. Teaching should exalt Christ and unite the church around the core doctrines of the faith.

Fellowship

The Holy Spirit equips believers with a variety of gifts. The Lord also created us with unique personalities, gave us stories, and united us together under the banner of Christ. The church should be a beautifully diverse mix of cultural backgrounds, personal stories, and experiences.

When Peter preached his sermon in Acts 2, the listening crowd was made up of ethnic Jews and non-Jewish converts to Judaism: "Parthians, Medes and Elamites; residents of Mesopotamia, Judea and Cappadocia, Pontus and Asia, Phrygia and Pamphylia, Egypt and the parts of Libya near Cyrene; visitors from Rome (both Jews and converts to Judaism); Cretans and Arabs—we hear them declaring the wonders of God in our own tongues!" (vv. 8–11).

From this crowd, three thousand people came to know Jesus. That means the early church was a mix of many different cultures, traditions, and even political affiliations. Chances are relationships were as hard then as they are now! The early Christians fellowshipped in unity, and their unity was one of their "lights" to the world.

The word *fellowship* is taken from the Greek *koinonia*, which means to "hold something in common," and reflects the shared beliefs, convictions, and behaviors of Christians.[6] Christians should unite around the essential doctrines of the faith (what you are learning in this book!) and give grace for differences of practice.

Theologian Rupertus Meldenius famously said, "In essentials, unity; in nonessentials, liberty; in all things, charity."[7] This is the foundation of healthy Christian fellowship: the ability to unite around the essentials of our faith, give grace for different expressions of Christianity, and gently correct our sisters when necessary. Healthy fellowship is vulnerable, loving, truthful, and wise.

Worship

When you hear the word *worship*, does your mind go to singing? The modern church equates the two. While singing is an expression of worship, worship encompasses much more. The ritual sacrifices of the Old Testament were worship. The gathering of Israel to honor the festivals and law was worship. *Worship* can be defined as attributing honor, attention, reverence, and focus to God.

Worship can and should be individual. Your work can be worship. You can worship through prayer, worship in your car, and worship as you rock babies. But worship should also be corporate. In the early church the worship services followed a Jewish model (since the early church was mostly Jewish) of prayer, praise, and scriptural study. All three were considered a form of worship because all three directed reverence toward God.

The most distinctive form of Christian worship are the sacraments. *Sacrament* comes from a Latin root for *oath* or *vow*. In the sixteenth century the Council of Trent called these "a visible sign of invisible grace."[8] The Catholic and Orthodox Churches observe seven sacraments, with some variation in their traditions:

- Baptism: a sacrament of sanctifying grace from original sin
- Confirmation: how admission to the church (via baptism) is confirmed
- Eucharist: a sacrament to commemorate the new covenant in bread and wine
- Reconciliation: confession for grace to cover ongoing sins
- Anointing the sick: sacramental comfort in suffering or preparation for death
- Matrimony: covenantal union between Christians representing Christ and the church
- Holy orders: the sacrament through which Christ's mission is imparted to ministers (ordination of priests)

These are organized into three sections. The first three are sacraments of Christian initiation, or introduction to the body of Christ. The next two are sacraments of healing relationally (reconciliation) or physically (anointing the sick). The final two are sacraments of commitment, whether in a covenant of marriage or commitment to ministry.

The Protestant church generally observes only two sacraments: baptism and Communion. Some non-Catholic churches may observe a few more, but these two are the standard. The Protestant

Reformers (Luther, Zwingli, and others) believed Jesus only insti-
tuted these two sacraments (Matthew 28:19; Luke 22:19) and that
the other five, while important to church life, were not expressly
commanded by Jesus and therefore cannot rightly be held to the
same level of importance. Some churches fall between Catholic
and Protestant in terms of what, or how many, sacraments they
observe.

Whatever our church tradition, these rituals of worship should
not be taken lightly. Though they don't save us (Christ does), they
are more than just symbols of the salvation story. Scripture and
church history testify to the importance of sacraments and how the
story they tell directs our hearts toward the God who saved us.

Perhaps our hearts need that direction toward reverence. We can
truthfully say the words of the old hymn, "Prone to wander, Lord, I
feel it."[9] When our minds wander during a group worship gathering,
it's worth asking, To what other things do I attribute honor, attention, and focus? It is sobering to recognize how often we "worship"
our concerns, fears, money, and relationships.

I find my mind wandering to these areas of life during church
services; perhaps that isn't a coincidence. At the moment our minds
could be fixed in worship alongside our Christian family, they
want to be filled with anything else! Worshiping together resets our
attention each week so we "[fix] our eyes on Jesus, the pioneer and
perfecter of faith. For the joy set before him he endured the cross,
scorning its shame, and sat down at the right hand of the throne of
God" (Hebrews 12:2).

Service

The church at Ephesus struggled to put others first. Husbands
and wives struggled. Masters and slaves struggled. Parents and children struggled. When Paul wrote his letter to the Ephesians, he
emphasized the importance of service, love, and respect. But before

he even addressed those issues, he cut to the heart of all the issues they were dealing with: "We are God's handiwork, created in Christ Jesus to do good works, which God prepared in advance for us to do" (Ephesians 2:10).

We aren't just called to do good works; we were *created* for them. Our new natures in Christ Jesus have a purpose—and that purpose is service. This shouldn't come as a surprise! Jesus himself "did not come to be served, but to serve, and to give his life as a ransom for many" (Matthew 20:28).

The gifts granted to us by the Spirit equip us to serve our Christian family. Peter advised his fledgling church, "Each of you should use whatever gift you have received to serve others, as faithful stewards of God's grace in its various forms" (1 Peter 4:10). He drew a parallel between faithful stewardship of salvation and our service to others. He expected disciples to put others before themselves.

We might use our spiritual gifts to be hospitable or to organize and lead. We might share a musical talent or a love for children. Our individual strengths guide us to the places the church and world need us most. Sometimes service is inconvenient and hard, but the Bible makes it clear that serving the church is not just for paid ministry staff; it is for the whole body of Christ.

This is a hard teaching in today's consumer culture. Many Christians attend church for what they "get": good music, a nice teaching, a social outing, and muffins. When one, or all, is subpar, they become disenchanted and leave. Church to them isn't a place to connect and serve. It's a commodity to consume. This could not be further from the New Testament model.

While we are encouraged to check a church's teaching and structure against Scripture, we are not encouraged to be hypercritical or consumeristic. What if we adopted Jesus' attitude and came "not to be served but to serve"? We might steward God's grace with greater faithfulness.

Evangelism

The final ministry of the church is evangelism.

Did your chest tighten when you read that word? Perhaps you had visions of gospel tracts, door-to-door cold calls, and spring break mission trips to a Miami beach. Evangelism makes us sweat because we often try to do it in our own wisdom and strength. We operate from a sense of anxious urgency rather than allowing God to lead.

Here's a freeing truth: evangelism comes naturally when we've experienced the richness of Christ! The gospel is beautiful, compelling, and encouraging. When we live in such a reality, sharing the faith isn't scary. It's just the overflow of a heart exposed to Jesus. Does anyone have to force us to talk about our favorite TV shows, recipes, or coffee orders? Of course not! We're quick to proclaim things that positively impact our lives. Jesus has had the most powerful impact on who we are. As we live into this truth, we will naturally share about His influence.

That said, evangelism isn't emotion-driven. The Spirit gives us the words by calling to mind the truths we've absorbed—and we need to do the work of absorbing them. Exposing ourselves to the Word of God, personally and in community, gives us the equipment to steward tough theological questions. Studying theological books, reading good articles, talking to your pastoral team—all these things equip you to engage with your culture's skepticism. We need intellectual equipping as well as spiritual.

Evangelism is also *relational*. Our vertical relationship with God, Jesus, and the Holy Spirit bubbles over to our horizontal relationships with people. Healthy personal relationships in church bolster our confidence when sharing our faith. Growing personal relationships with unbelievers grants us opportunities to pour the love of Christ into hearts who don't know Him.

Evangelism ministry requires spiritual maturity, intellectual pursuit, and emotional health, but it is driven by a deep, abiding love for Jesus. People who've met Jesus and know how good He is can't help but tell the world about Him. The church should be filled with such people, and until it is, may we become the kind of Christians whose affection for God can't be contained.

When Church Hurts

My earliest memories are from a church sanctuary. It doubled as a school gym, scent and all, with ceilings stretching tall above my first-grade head, hung with the flags of at least twenty different nations. "Reminds us to pray for the world," Dad said when I asked why they were there.

It was a vibrant church: singing, dancing (people danced!), and most of all the way people loved one another. Even at a young age, I could see it. I thought my parents' friends were old; now I know they couldn't have been older than thirty-two. They'd all attended one another's weddings in the years before and after I was born. Their kids were my "fake cousins"; I called the parents "aunt" and "uncle." By the time I was ten, I had no less than eight sets of pseudo-relatives.

But when I was twelve, the church went through a devastating split. Members scattered to different churches in the area when reconciliation couldn't be reached. The late-night talks, which were whispered upstairs when I was supposed to be sleeping, the phone calls and meetings, the struggle to discern the right path—even at my young age I could see the pain. And we felt it. Our friends, our family, now went to a different church. We began a yearslong journey of finding a new home church in a spiritually dry part of the country. It was hard.

The people on both sides of that church split were good people. They were and are Christ followers who love Him and live faithful lives. But like all churches, ours was full of sanctified sinners. Sinners will inevitably hurt one another. They will offend with pride, jealousy, selfishness, and anger. Christians are called to pursue unity, but unity takes work. And sometimes unity can't be achieved.

Church hurts because people hurt. We bring our raw, wounded selves, our childhood experiences, our theological biases, and sometimes our consumer mindsets to a gathering of other similarly flawed people and expect unity. Perhaps the apostles preached unity as much as they did because they *knew* it would take so much work. They knew we would offend and forgive and offend and forgive again. They knew we would wrestle with emotionally unhealthy people and spiritually immature ones.

They knew, because they wrestled too:

> Who is wise and understanding among you? By his good conduct let him show his works in the meekness of wisdom. But if you have bitter jealousy and selfish ambition in your hearts, do not boast and be false to the truth. This is not the wisdom that comes down from above, but is earthly, unspiritual, demonic. For where jealousy and selfish ambition exist, there will be disorder and every vile practice. (James 3:13–16 ESV)

I think it's safe to say James was dealing with people who were jealous and selfish. He didn't mince words: this kind of behavior is demonic. It's demonic because it is anti-unity, anti-peace, anti-love—in other words, anti-Christ. And to be anti-Christ is to align with the Accuser. James dealt with people who were choosing a dark and deadly way. Paul must have too; he warned the church at Philippi against the same things:

> Do nothing from selfish ambition or conceit, but in humility count others more significant than yourselves. Let each of you look not only to his own interests, but also to the interests of others. (Philippians 2:3–4 ESV)

Rivalry, conceit, jealousy, selfish ambition. These are church-wreckers. And if you've been part of a local gathering of believers for a significant amount of time, you've probably faced them. When iron sharpens iron, sparks fly (Proverbs 27:17). Those who are willing to be sharpened come out stronger and better for the experience. Those who resent repentance and the endurance of love (1 Corinthians 13:8) will come out bitter and angry. We get to choose which Christian we'll be.

When to Walk Away

The church split hurt our family and broke my parents' hearts, but over the years we recovered. The church recovered too. The friendships continued and many continue to this day. Our "church hurt" was painful, but it was not abusive, and the people involved were not hardened to the voice of God. They are followers of Jesus now as much as they were when we all worshiped under the same roof. But our story is not how every church experience goes.

It is important to distinguish between abusive church situations and Christian disagreement. With the latter, reconciliation may be possible. With the former, it's not always advised.

Spiritual abuse happens when leaders in the church act from authoritarian power rather than servant leadership.[10] Such leaders might gaslight people who disagree, stack their elder team with people who won't question them, use Scripture to support an agenda, and carefully manage their public image rather than live in transparent accountability. In such churches the pastor or organization takes priority over the people. Sometimes this results in failure to report to authorities on sexual or physical abuses within a church.

These kinds of church experiences can be more emotionally traumatic than a church split and can affect our view of God, ourselves, fellow Christians, and the global church. God has great compassion for those who experience abuse; Jesus rebuked people who justified their sin in the name of Scripture (Luke 11; Mark 9).

If you've experienced pain at the hands of a Christian leader or group, I am so sorry. God sees. He did not cause this, desire this, or endorse this. But He is ready to heal this! Healing from spiritual abuse takes time and requires separating God's character from the character of those who hurt you.

Rehearsing truth about the God who loves you may help form that distinction:

- God is compassionate, gracious, and just (Exodus 34:5–7).
- God loves justice and mercy (Micah 6:8).
- God thinks you are valuable (Matthew 6:26).
- God is a shield to those who take refuge in Him (Psalm 18:30).
- God is with you (Isaiah 41:10).

After rehearsing the truth, you will need to set boundaries with the church or abuser. Reach out to people you can trust to ask for support and perspective. Invite their prayers for wisdom, protection, and healing. You may even need to see a licensed counselor to continue processing and healing from what you experienced.

The global church contains humble, sincere, supportive Christians who do not treat others with dishonor and disrespect. There is hope for a local church family who exemplify a truly biblical ecclesiology!

Your Role in the Church

The home my dad built still stands today. It's been repainted, the landscaping redone; none of the interior rooms look like they did when I was a child. There are new owners living on the land where I ran barefoot to the garden and rode my pony bareback in the sun. Time has turned twenty years into a flash, but the house still stands. It has outlasted the first family who lived and loved within its walls. It lives to welcome others, people I will never know.

Like that house, the church has lived to welcome thousands of people into the family of God. It has outlasted the first family, the early church, and has grown into a worldwide embrace of all who call upon the name of the Lord to be saved (Romans 10:13). It lives on, year upon year, centuries stacking upon one another like foundation blocks as the gospel continues to transform hearts. It was never about the building, or the music, or the sermons. It still isn't. Church is about Holy Spirit-led people communing with God and one another.

Church is family, even when it hurts.

As Christians, we *are* the church. We must bear with the church, because that's love: to bear, to believe, to endure, to walk with those who imperfectly image Christ *just like we do*. To think we are beyond this is to misunderstand our own propensity to hurt and fail others. And with the average, daily difficulty of walking with fellow Christians who sin, we need the same patience God shows us.

Your role in the church cannot be underestimated. Whether you are leading college students, watching babies, running the soundboard, or yes, serving muffins, your service of fellow church members is a service for Christ. Every person who dedicates themselves to the family of God makes that family stronger, kinder, and healthier. The church needs you because the church *is* you—plus your brothers and sisters.

The city on a hill is built one person at a time, but it does not end with one person. We are little temples being built up into one united temple to God. When the world looks at the church—our collective body of believers in Jesus—they should see the fruit of Jesus' Spirit: love, joy, peace, patience, kindness, goodness, faithfulness, gentleness, and self-control. They should see our community redeeming the disunity of a broken world, offering a better way to live in relationship with one another. We the people of the church should be extending a branch of hope, because to be the church is to be hope realized, hope embodied a thousand times over.

PASTORS, ELDERS, AND BISHOPS, OH MY!

Not all churches are organized in the same manner. Some churches have a clear hierarchy (such as Roman Catholic and Orthodox) while others do not have central denominational authorities and are instead completely independent gatherings (such as Church of Christ and Mennonite). Other churches might have a "conference" of leaders, allowing freedom for churches in that conference to practice faith diversely as long as they adhere to the doctrinal statement of the denomination (Baptist and Methodist).

Churches may have pastors, elders, bishops, or some combination of both. Ever wonder what the difference is? *Pastor* was originally an adjective, not a title: it described what the head of the local church was doing. To pastor is to "shepherd" a group of people toward the Lord. Bishops were overseers of the church. Sometimes a bishop oversees multiple churches. The word *elder* originally referred to the older men in the Jewish community but came to mean a person of godly character who helps make governing decisions in the church (1 Timothy 5:17). Many churches have both pastors and elders, and some have bishops overseeing local church pastors who also have an elder team for accountability and decision-making.

Chapter 8

Eschatology: A New Heaven and a New Earth

THE DOCTRINE OF LAST THINGS

Red flowers nod gently in the wind, and I bend to cut the stems close to the ground, handing gladiolas to Adeline one at a time. We move to the zinnias, orange and yellow in their sunlike faces, until Adeline's hands are full to overflowing with the bright beauty of summer. By our feet, bush beans spill into the path between beds. Peas climb beyond their trellis; they never make it to the kitchen due to the constant snacking of little harvesters. I stand, hands on hips, looking across the hayfield where Farmer Bob's alfalfa sways green.

Is this what heaven is like?

The storybooks told us heaven would be a placid place of harps and angels. We've been told, "It will be like one long worship service, except we'll like it better—don't worry! You won't mind all the hymns and standing around for eternity." But deep down we know this can't be the truth about eternity. The first garden was full of purpose: Adam and Eve were tasked to care for the garden and work it. They were to take on God's creation and continue creating within it. Why then do we portray heaven as a place of perpetual inactivity?

When it comes to the last days of earth, we fear persecution and suffering. We worry over when Jesus will return and what kind of things will happen before He does. For most Christians, theology of the end times holds neither joy nor peace.

ESCHATOLOGY:
theology of the final things

Eschatology is the fancy word for "theology of the final things." It comes from two Greek words: *éschatos*, or "final," and *logos*, which means "word" or "idea." When we talk about eschatology, we're really talking about God bringing all things to reconciliation or justice. We glimpse God's intent for the final days throughout the Bible, but the last book in the New Testament tells us the most.

Revelation is the wild book at the end of the Bible with all the visions, the bowls, and the seals. Its account parallels truths we learn in the book of Daniel and in John 14, where Jesus talked about the end times. Together, these narratives shape our understanding of God's plan for the last days of the earth and the new world He will build in its stead.

Some of us might be confused between the biblical account of the end times and books and movies like *Left Behind*. This fictional book series describing the return of Christ was a bestseller in the nineties and early 2000s. It was so popular that its impact on Christian eschatology is felt to this day.

Many Christians consider the return of Christ an event laden with fear and anxiety, not joy and victory. But the return of our Savior, the second coming of the Messiah, should not be an event full of fear. We must align our view of end times with what Scripture teaches and learn how Christians have interpreted it over the years. It may surprise you to learn that all Christians do not interpret the passages about end times the same way.

The End of Life As We Know It

Knowing that life will one day end is difficult to comprehend. There is a sense of trepidation at the unknown of it all. But God is compassionate to our humanity, and He intentionally revealed His purposes in Scripture as an encouragement for us to persevere.

The message of Revelation is not "be afraid!" but "*do not* be afraid" (Revelation 1:17, emphasis added). Wrestling with our view of the end times is one of the most beneficial spiritual tasks we can undertake. Coming to terms with Revelation's message and accepting God's narrative of love frees us to view the end of days with peace.

To begin this journey, we must diversify the voices we listen to regarding end times theology. There are four primary views on the end times, each held at different points in church history and most still entertained by scholars today. The goal of studying these views is to open our minds to different explanations of Christ's return. Much of what is said in the Bible about the final days is in nuanced language involving symbolism, imagery, and numbers. The more we understand the intent of the authors and the significance of such symbolism in other parts of the Bible, the better we can understand Revelation.

We tend to look at our current circumstances through our eschatological lens. Christians who believe God is about to remove Christians from the world and that persecution is increasing have a different view of our current circumstances than the Christians who believe persecution affects the world in cycles. How we perceive world events affects our emotional reaction to those events and even our life choices within them. How important it is to wrestle with our eschatology!

Before we discuss the four end times views, let's look at some terms scholars use when discussing them. These terms summarize the ideas we find in the biblical text.

- *Church age*: The church age is the era or span of time from the beginning of the church to present day. This time frame spans from Jesus' ascension right around AD 30–33 to the final things, which Jesus predicted (John 14).
- *The first coming of Christ*: The first coming is when Jesus initially entered the world, born of a virgin, and lived on earth from about 4 BC to AD 30.
- *The second coming of Christ*: This is the bodily return of Jesus as King. Across all of the views of the second coming, it is agreed that Jesus will be actually returning to earth to rule and reign and conquer evil for good.
- *Millennial reign*: The millennium, or millennial reign, is a thousand-year period when Jesus will reign on earth as described in Revelation 20. There are different perspectives on what this millennium means and will look like.
- *Preterist*: This refers to biblical prophecies about the end times applying to past events. At the time of the writing of Revelation, these events would have been in the future. But for us today, these events are now in the past. A preterist would see references to the Antichrist as references to Emperor Nero; the tribulation would be the Jewish war; and the abominations include things like the destruction of the temple, which happened in AD 70. A preterist believes John's prophecies were fulfilled in the first century of the church.
- *Futurist*: This view of the end times believes all the events described are yet to occur and will still happen in the future. This is the view of premillennial Christians, who believe Christ's millennial earthly reign is yet to happen.
- *Historicist*: This view holds that the events in Revelation

depict the arc of church history from the apostles' day to ours. The wars, bloodshed, and persecution we see in Revelation all occurred in the two thousand years between John's vision and today.

- *Idealist*: Popularized by early church fathers Origen and Augustine, this view holds that Revelation does not have to do with historical events at all but is instead symbolic of the battle between God and Satan, good and evil. God's victory at the end represents our hope in Christ.
- *Tribulation*: A period of persecution prophesied about in Revelation. Some believe this is a specific and literal span of time; others believe persecution comes in cycles represented in Scripture through symbolic language.

These terms help put a label on the theological principles we learn in the book of Revelation and other passages in Scripture. Sometimes fellow believers will use these terms to describe their position on the end times, so understanding them equips us for conversation.

Symbolism and Apocalyptic Literature

It was almost midnight that Santa Fe summer. After an ice cream stop at the square, my friends and I were packed into my red PT Cruiser. We had to be back at our camp by curfew to prepare for another day of coaching campers, but Santa Fe's roads are notoriously confusing.

"I think it's this way," I muttered, turning right out of the downtown area, creeping toward the mountain. The road was dark, my friends were loud, and I was a bit distracted. I didn't see the flashing lights until I was upon them. With a *thump thump* I revved the Cruiser and made it just under the descending railroad bars.

"Did you just . . . did you just drive in front of a *train*?" one of my friends gasped from the passenger seat. And, yes, she should have been gasping—the train was on her side of the car.

"I . . . I . . . guess so?" I gripped the steering wheel as the adrenaline caught up with me. *I can't believe I just did that.* The car was quiet. Then it burst into unbelieving laughs.

"Are you trying to *kill us*? Haven't you ever seen a train crossing before?"

Truth was, I really hadn't. There were no trains in my little Michigan town. The only time we had to watch the train crossing was once a year when the Artrain came up from downstate. I didn't know the symbol for train crossing, and in the moment I didn't even recall that *red* means *stop*. I was unfamiliar with the symbolism, so I missed the meaning—and endangered us all.

EXEGESIS: *drawing out the intended and accurate meaning of a text*

The Bible is full of symbolism, but Revelation maximizes its use. These symbols give us hints and parallels by which to discern the author's intent. These symbols are used and recognized in Jewish literature as well as Christian. When we don't understand the symbolism, or intentionally create our own meanings for it, we endanger the message of the text. Since biblical theology depends on proper exegesis (discerning the meaning of the text), reviewing some of this symbolism is helpful.

Here are a few examples from Revelation itself:

- moon under a woman's feet: symbolic of dominion
- crown: symbolic of royalty
- horns: symbols of power
- heads: symbols of authority
- diadems: symbol of government
- seven: symbol of perfection or completion
- twelve stars: usually refers either to the Old Testament

"church" (tribes of Israel) or the New Testament church (represented by the twelve apostles)

The most famous symbol in Revelation is the "mark of the Beast," signified by the number "666." There has been much speculation about what "666" represents. In both Hebrew and Greek, numbers can be written as letters. The numbers could represent the numeric value of a name. Some scholars suggest it represents the Roman Empire or one of its leaders, such as Nero, who persecuted the church. Other suggestions are almost endless. The pope, communism, Hillary Clinton, Donald Trump, and most recently Joe Biden have all been pinpointed as possible antichrists. But finding the antichrist is not the purpose of this passage of Revelation.

Since the number seven represents completion, the number six "falls short," representing incompletion. The number 666 means *everything opposite of God* and might simply represent the unholy trinity of dragon, beast, and the beast's spokesperson in Revelation 13.

We live in the age of information. We are constantly assaulted with memes, news reports, and videos depicting the darkest stories of the world. We're also exposed to a variety of Christian opinions about those events. The symbolism of Revelation is sometimes employed to explain or interpret the trials of this world. By understanding what these symbols meant for the readers in John's day, we're better equipped to discern current events and whether they are "fulfillments" of Revelation prophecy.

Four Views of the End Times

I've given you a lot of terminology, and I promise you'll use it! These terms play a part in the four theological views of end times. These four views teach that the final things will play out in distinctly different ways, but each view is identified by its interpretation of the millennium.

Premillennial Christians believe the millennium is a future event and Jesus will return before it happens. *Amillennial* Christians believe the millennium is just a symbol of Christ's present reign among His people. (*A-millennial* means "no millennium.") *Postmillennial* means Jesus will return after the millennial reign, a thousand-year period in which most of the world submits to Jesus. Amillennial and postmillennial Christians both tend to be preterists, believing the events of Revelation occurred mostly in the past. Premillennial Christians are futurists, believing the events will occur in the future.

As we look at these four views, think about the present-day impact each one might have. How would this view change how you interact with current events? With your community? With your faith? Our eschatology changes us. So spend some time thinking about how these eschatological views might change you.

Historical/Covenant Premillennialism

Historical premillennialism was the view of the early church fathers. While it may be tempting to think this means "more accurate," keep in mind that the church fathers were not infallible. They were a product of their time just like every scholar since. Understanding their view gives us a glimpse of what the church believed in the early years, but even then many scholars disagreed on the details of these views.

Another word for historical premillennialism is *covenant premillennialism*. The early fathers believed the thousand-year reign would be a literal future event; Jesus Christ would come and reign on the earth. But as the church fathers died and as Greek philosophy began to influence the church, the physical world became perceived as less important than the spiritual realm. The idea of an actual millennium and physical reign of Jesus on earth began to fade.

The early church fathers believed that the promises to the nation of Israel were fulfilled by the church. This meant Israel would no longer inherit God's promises because of their disobedience to God and rejection of the Messiah. So the church fathers understood references to Israel as symbolic of the church, or the "spiritual Israel."

The church fathers took this view from First and Second Thessalonians, Galatians, Jeremiah, and Romans as well as their own experience with (and sometimes bias against) the Jews. We must remember there was animosity between the Jews and the Christians in the early years, and it went both ways. Some Christians were sinfully anti-Semitic, believing the Jews were responsible for killing Christ rather than recognizing all of humanity was responsible. On the other hand, Jews were very offended to see Christians "co-opting" the Jews' legacy and incorporating Jesus, who they did not believe was the Messiah. The conflict between the two groups eventually resulted in the separate church holidays we see today (Easter instead of Passover, for example).

Historic premillennialism is *futurist* in its view of Revelation.

Amillennialism

As mentioned earlier, *amillennialism* literally means "no millennium." To amillennial Christians, the millennium is symbolic: the spiritual reign of Jesus in the hearts of His followers. Christ's triumph over Satan restrained the power of Satan on earth. There will always be persecution of Christians, but Jesus is reigning spiritually right now. When He finally returns physically in the second coming, He will defeat evil for good. Up to that point we're experiencing tribulation.

Amillennialism is distinctive because tribulation or persecution is happening at the same time as Christ's reign. Picture the cross as our starting point, almost like a timeline. Christ is reigning and, at the same time, tribulation and persecution are happening like a parallel line to Christ's work in the world.

If we look at history, that is exactly what has happened. Christians have been persecuted on and off and in different areas of the world for the entirety of the church age. So, in this church age, according to the amillennial view, Christ is winning people to Him, taking them into the body of Christ, as tribulation and trial are happening at the same time. When Christ finally returns, all things will be made right, and we will join in the new heaven and the new earth He is creating.

This view became popular in the fifth century as the historical premillennial view waned. It may have been influenced by a Greek philosophy that didn't put as much emphasis on the physical as it did the spiritual (like premillennialism did), but it can be argued biblically as well. Amillennial believers do not take the numbers and symbols as literal explanations but as representative of a spiritual reality. The Bible does use the number "one thousand" figuratively (Psalm 50; Psalm 90; Psalm 105; and 2 Peter 3), which may support the idea of a symbolic millennial reign.

Amillennialism is either *preterist* or *historicist* in its view of Revelation.

Postmillennialism

The postmillennial view is that the second coming of Christ will happen after the thousand-year reign of Christ. There will be a church age followed by a tribulation period when evil forces will be at work in the world. Gradually, as Christians expose the world to the gospel, the world will get better. Postmillennials think the world is going to improve over time as the world is won to the gospel, and Christ will return once all the people who need to be saved are brought into the church.

This view of the end times is probably the least common view among Christians. We see it in some Calvinistic Christian groups and also among charismatic churches.

In charismatic or Pentecostal churches, *postmillennialism* is sometimes called *dominion postmillennialism*. In this tradition Christians believe that God is binding Satan, and as the church recognizes its power and walks in the Holy Spirit, the world will improve.

Dispensational Premillennialism

While *premillennialism* may sound intimidating, this is likely the eschatology with which you are most familiar, even if you don't have words for it. The premillennial viewpoint is the one popularized by the Left Behind series. However, it's not a stand-alone view; it comes from dispensational theology, which is why the more accurate term for this end times perspective is *dispensational premillennialism*.

To put it simply, dispensationalism is a *framework* for understanding the history of God's interaction with humanity. It is not the only framework, but it became popular in the mid-1800s. Dispensational theology breaks the Bible up into seven eras, or dispensations. God reveals Himself differently in each of these eras. We are currently in the "dispensation of grace" through Christ, and Revelation depicts the final dispensation: the kingdom of God and restoration of Israel.

Before I explain further, let's recap what we have learned so far.

Historical premillennialism says, "The church age is happening, society is growing evil, there's a great persecution. Christ returns, He reigns in an actual thousand-year millennium, and then all things are restored." Pretty straightforward.

The amillennial view is even more straightforward: "Jesus came, He died, He ascended, and the church age happened. Believers are persecuted the entire time, and then Jesus returns."

The postmillennial view works like this: "The church age resulted in a society gradually improving, a final persecution, and Jesus returns." Again, very simple.

But with dispensational premillennialism, everything is a little more complicated. This is consistent with how dispensationalism views the entire biblical narrative. This view was popularized by a scholar named C.I. Scofield, who wrote *The Scofield Reference Bible*, which makes it rather new to church history at less than two hundred years old. *The Scofield Reference Bible* was sent to all the major seminaries in the continental US and shaped the views of pastors for a century, including their views on the end times. It made dispensational premillennial views popular, especially among American fundamentalist Baptist churches. Most non-Calvinist churches were eventually exposed to this theology and many embraced it. Dispensational premillennialism took the world by storm.

Premillennialism differs from the other views by taking a futuristic and literal approach to Revelation. Premillennial Christians believe Jesus will come back to earth after a seven-year tribulation and will rule from Jerusalem during a literal thousand years of peace on earth.

Israel is a centerpiece of premillennial theology: rather than continue the work of Israel through the church, premillennial Christians believe the political state of Israel still has a role to play in God's plan for last things. They view the regathering of Israel as a recognized state in the 1940s as a significant fulfillment of prophecy. This view expanded among Christians and was popularized by teachers like Hal Lindsey, Chuck Smith, Charles Ryrie, Tim LaHaye (author of the Left Behind series), and John MacArthur.

Though all four views agree on Jesus' second coming, only dispensationalists believe in a rapture of the church. The rapture describes a sudden event where Christians are "taken up" out of the world into the heavenly places (1 Thessalonians 4:15–17). The rapture and the second coming of Jesus are two separate events. The concept of a rapture is a very recent doctrine, nonexistent in church history up until the 1800s. It's taken from 1 Thessalonians 4:

> This we declare to you by a word from the Lord, that we who are alive, who are left until the coming of the Lord, will not

precede those who have fallen asleep. For the Lord himself will descend from heaven with a cry of command, with the voice of an archangel, and with the sound of the trumpet of God. And the dead in Christ will rise first. Then we who are alive, who are left, will be caught up together with them in the clouds to meet the Lord in the air, and so we will always be with the Lord. (vv. 15–17 ESV)

This being "caught up in the air" was taken to mean the rapture of the church out of the world.

Though Christians disagree on whether a rapture can truly be argued from Scripture, there is one thing we know for sure: the Bible does not teach a "secret" or "silent" rapture. First Thessalonians 4 says there will be a great shout and a trumpet sound when the church meets Christ. The scriptural rapture will be a public event.

Premillennials are also the only Christians who debate whether a rapture will occur pre-tribulation or post-tribulation—in other words, whether God will take Christians out of the world before or after a great persecution. The other three views don't enter this debate because they believe tribulation occurs simultaneously with the reign of Christ, and the rapture is not part of their doctrine.

Because of how structured dispensational theology is, the story of Revelation is broken into distinct sections: there will be a great tribulation, a second coming of Christ, and then the millennial reign, after which there will be a final judgment. When it comes to the significant numbers we see in Revelation—a seven-year tribulation, the thousand-year millennial reign, 666—an amillennial Christian interprets those symbolically while a dispensational premillennialist takes them literally. This affects their interpretation of the text as well.

Premillennialism can be a very hopeful way to live. Seeing Revelation as a futuristic event can be an encouragement to live with urgency for the gospel. However, fear and anxiety have no place in the Christian view of the end times. Revelation is a book of promise and victory. It was given to us for eternal hope and encouragement to finish our faith well. It's also important to recognize that our view of the end times, while important, does not make or break our Christianity. Two Christians can be faithful believers and arrive at different conclusions about the final things.

The Love of God's Wrath

There is one last thing we're going to reckon with in Revelation, and that's the judgment of God. There are judgments of every size and shape: bowls, seals, trumpets, horsemen, bloody battles. It has all the makings of an R-rated movie. There's even a prostitute named Babylon riding a horned beast with wine in her hand. Crazy stuff!

Christians often pit God and Jesus against each other. God is judgment, wrath, and anger; Jesus is kindness and love. We dealt with this in the soteriology chapter, but as a reminder, Jesus is the *expression* of God's love. Jesus would not have come if it were not God's loving plan (John 3:16), and He always did the will of the Father (John 6:38). Jesus said that He and the Father are one (John 10:30).

The wrath of God, then, is the wrath of Christ; and the love of Christ is the love of God.

Sometimes, the more familiar we are with the Bible, the more flippant we become. Instead our familiarity with God should bring a greater sense of wonder and awe. Who is this God, so holy and unapproachable, who made Himself approachable for us?

We cannot forget this truth as we look at the judgments of Revelation and the justice of final things. As we read about the seal, trumpet, and bowl judgments, it can be easy to think primarily of God's anger and forget about His love—or even question His love.

But God's love and grace exist *because* He is just and holy. Without His justice—calling evil to account—there would be no need for grace. Without His judging evil for the wreckage it creates in human lives and hearts, we could not fully experience love. God's love and justice are not opposites; they are two sides of the same coin. You can't have one without the other.

"Though I used to complain about the indecency of the idea of God's wrath," wrote theologian Mirosav Volf, "I came to think that I would have to rebel against a God who wasn't wrathful at the sight of the world's evil. God isn't wrathful in spite of being love. God is wrathful because God is love."[1]

War, bloodshed, abuse, molestation, deceit, corruption: God's judgments call *all* of these to account. Both the preterist (Revelation is past) and the futurist (Revelation is future) can agree that God's template is one of loving justice. He makes right the wrongs of sinful humans.

Scholar William Barclay put it this way: "The wrath of God is the wrath of love, which is not out to destroy, but even in anger, is out to save those whom it loves."[2]

God's wrath is His love on display. The love of God defending His image bearers from every evil thing, purifying the world, driving out the darkness—including any and all who align with it. God's justice is a comfort, because the unrighteous things we have seen in our lives on earth will be brought to a just and righteous end.

As fallible humans, we cannot pick and choose who is held accountable and who is not. How quickly would we make excuses for sin just to accomplish our ends! No, we must trust the holiness and justice of God. And we must remember that only in our triune God does justice exist *because* of love and not without it. Other religions possess gods who are just, but not loving. They have no framework of grace.

Over and over thus far we have seen how easy it is to be part of the protected, sealed children of God. *Just turn to Christ!* Those who choose not to do so choose to stay under wrath—a destiny God never wanted for them, but that He will not stop them from choosing for themselves.

What an urgency we have for people to know this God! Who could be greater than the One who loves so deeply and goes to such ends? He opens wide the door of heaven because He does not wish for any to perish but for all to come to repentance (2 Peter 3:9). The grace of God has revealed Jesus Christ to offer all people a chance to know Him, to spend eternity with Him, to restore the brokenness that Eden introduced.

Nothing Left but Resurrection

It's a Sunday in March, the garden buried beneath a layer of snow. We're all pressed around Grandpa and Grandma's table, a card table jammed up to the end with a piano stool and pillows stacked up for the toddlers. We squish together, passing around orange Jell-O and coconut ice cream and the birthday cake. Another birthday without my uncle there. Another sitting at a table with a seat unfilled. Another moment of happy-brokenness, another reminder of the family we are and the Family he's with now.

We thank You for this food and the blessing of family, that we can gather here in Your name. Grandpa pauses his prayer. *We miss Matt.* There is a tremor in his voice, in us. *Thank You that the best is yet to come.*

It's the same phrase my grandpa uses to sign all his letters: *The best is yet to come.*

And it is.

Where does grief go for people of resurrection? It cannot rest in empty words; it cannot abide pithy platitudes. There must be a hope better than what the world can offer. No one can replace the loved ones lost. No one can heal the jagged scars of this world, the jagged scars of the heart. Where is the reckoning with all this pain?

There is but one reckoning and one only: the cross. At the cross God grieved the pain of a million lives, felt the weight of ten thousand burdens, cried the tears of every child, man, and woman who called out for justice, for freedom, for love. The reckoning has occurred. All that is left . . . is resurrection.

> To grieve with hope
> a love with nowhere to go
> must meet the Love that will not let us go,
> and there, so slowly,
> the grieving heart
> finds final home.

Jesus rose from the dead as a promise: we, too, will one day rise with Him. Death is not the end for us, and because of this, death has lost its sting (1 Corinthians 15:55). He is making all things—us, the earth, life as we know it—new.

A New Heaven and a New Earth

It's hard to imagine a world made completely new. We have no framework for a world without our history of death, pain, and sorrow. Every civilization bears the mark of suffering. And yet this newness is exactly what God promises:

> Then I saw "a new heaven and a new earth," for the first heaven
> and the first earth had passed away, and there was no longer any
> sea. I saw the Holy City, the new Jerusalem, coming down out of
> heaven from God, prepared as a bride beautifully dressed for her

husband. And I heard a loud voice from the throne saying, "Look! God's dwelling place is now among the people, and he will dwell with them. They will be his people, and God himself will be with them and be their God." (Revelation 21:1–3)

Here we have a great reversal of Babel and Babylon's way: Instead of a people striving to build a city to heaven, God lowers a city down to them. *God's dwelling place is now among the people.* Eden returns.

This was God's intent all along—to be with His people. He dwelt with Noah in the ark. He dwelt with Moses in the tabernacle. He dwelt with Solomon in the temple. He dwells with us today through the Holy Spirit. But in the last days He will dwell with us in all His glory—no walls, no rituals, no barriers. No death, no mourning, no pain, for the old order of things will have passed away (Revelation 21:4). In that day a new earth will be given, one unmarred by the pain of the past. We will dwell in peace with one another, peace with God, peace with ourselves.

Because the new world will have no barriers between humanity and God, there will be no need for a physical temple:

I did not see a temple in the city, because the Lord God Almighty and the Lamb are its temple. The city does not need the sun or the moon to shine on it, for the glory of God gives it light, and the Lamb is its lamp. (Revelation 21:22–23)

These imperfect temples God chooses to dwell in and this imperfect temple of the church will be "consummated" in the marriage of Christ and the church. We will dwell in the actual presence of God at full glory, and we will not turn away: "For now we see in a mirror dimly, but then face to face" (1 Corinthians 13:12 ESV).

This, my friends, is our hope. This was the hope of the Christian martyrs and missionaries, the hope of every Christ follower before us. We do not follow Jesus for fear of hell but for the joy set before us—for eternity with Him! It is far easier to look forward to eternity in Christ when you have experienced the greatness of Christ on earth.

This new world may not be much different from the current one—just without the pain and suffering. There will be nations and kings (Revelation 21:24). We will probably work in the kingdom like Adam and Eve worked the garden, but there will not be the resistance of sin. All the best things of this world plus all the goodness of perfection—this is heaven! We can put aside the boring pictures of harps and cupids because just as life in Christ is an adventure now, it is sure to be an adventure later.

A biblical eschatology is a hopeful eschatology. We are already part of the story God is writing. We can trust there is a good ending.

The best is yet to come.

MARK OF THE LORD

The mark of the Beast has been many things: tattoos, a microchip, and even a vaccine. But did you know the "mark of the Beast" isn't the only mark in Revelation? There is a far more important mark that Christians almost never talk about, and it's found in Revelation 7:3-4: the mark of God. This mark is given to a group of 144,000 people. In the spiritual interpretation—largely held by amillennial theologians—the number 144,000 represents the whole of God's people: twelve for the tribes of Israel, twelve for the apostles (leaders of the church), and 1,000 for completeness. The concept here is *God's protection of His own*. Persecution is promised, but the seal is also a promise—an assurance— that God will see His people through.

The Beast's people are marked by their alignment with him and are therefore sealed for destruction; God's people are marked with the blood of Jesus and are sealed in Christ forever. And good news: according to

Ephesians 1:13–14, the seal of Christ is the Spirit! Christians are marked by the presence of the Holy Spirit, their Comforter, Advocate, and sanctifier. And by this Spirit, God promises to watch over His own, even when they face trial and persecution. We are "marked" with Christ's righteousness, His identity, and His Spirit. The knowledge that we are sealed by God should remove anxiety about the final things.

Conclusion

O n a Thursday, in a brick café in Michigan, theology once again became essential.

Now eight years later, I leaned over a café miel and looked into the eyes of a new friend. This friend had questions of her own—wrestlings with God and evil. I saw her heart. And I knew the truth. Isn't that the intersection for true theologians? Reach the heart; hold the truth.

You've certainly had a whirlwind introduction to Christian theology in this book. You probably won't retain all of it. That's okay because this is just the beginning of your journey! Theology becomes real when it is ingrained into our being—when the truths about God and Christ and the Spirit become not just facts we *know* but realities we *live*.

The goal of this information is not to bludgeon people with facts or compare notes and make lists of people who don't measure up to our standards. The goal is for us to develop a reasoned faith, to employ heart, soul, *and* mind in pursuit of our Savior. The result of this pursuit is Christian maturity:

Anyone who lives on milk, being still an infant, is not acquainted with the teaching about righteousness. But solid food is for the mature, who by constant use have trained themselves to distinguish good from evil. Therefore let us move beyond the elementary teachings about Christ and be taken forward to maturity . . . (Hebrews 5:13–6:1)

Milk—easy, foundational teachings about Jesus—is good for baby Christians. But eventually we have to grow up. We have to be trained to "distinguish good from evil." This practice is called *discernment*. In the years I've led Every Woman a Theologian, I've found that the best way to teach discernment is not to scare people with all the false teachings about Christ; it's to educate them in the *right* teachings about Christ. As some say: know the original so well you aren't fooled by the fake.

The right or sound teachings about Christianity are called *orthodoxy*. The right practice of those teachings is called *orthopraxy*. We need both to be effective and holy witnesses for Christ in the world.

I love G. K. Chesterton's definition of orthodoxy. He said that orthodoxy is the creeds and the historic behavior of those who followed such a creed (such as the Apostles' Creed, which we studied early in this book).[1] Basically, what we see outlined by the church are the fundamentals of Christian belief and Christian practice. What behaviors were followed? How did they live? What kind of practices in their communities showed their values?

ORTHODOXY: *right or sound teachings about Christianity*

ORTHOPRAXY: *right practice of Christianity*

The pursuit of orthodoxy is a key to being "taken forward to maturity." Our training in discernment enables us to tell when something aligns with core Christian teachings and when it doesn't. And if this discernment is rooted in a strong personal relationship with Christ, we'll be sensitive to when our orthopraxy is falling short—when we aren't living what we believe. The tagline of Every Woman a Theologian is "know what you believe, and live it boldly." Knowing the orthodox way is not enough; we must live it out with grace.

The Rise of the Ungracious Christian

Living graciously is much harder than it sounds. When Christians first dive into theology, knowledge feels like power. Suddenly we have an ability to recognize why certain teachings are unbiblical! These young believers can fall into the trap of becoming "theological guard dogs," lecturing anyone who will listen about the errant teachings of *this* pastor or *that* Instagram account. Because they are still in the process of being "trained to distinguish between good and evil," they sometimes misconstrue core Christian doctrines—orthodoxy—with issues of freedom. They elevate things like worship music, dress codes, and Bible translations to the same importance as the resurrection and virgin birth of Christ.

When left unchecked this lack of discernment gives rise to a new brand of ungracious Christians. These Christians deceive themselves into thinking they are "loving" because they speak "the truth," but their tone is sarcastic, condescending, and angry, and their "truth" revolves around issues of preference, not core doctrines of the faith.

"Dear friends, let us love one another, for love comes from God," the apostle John wrote. "Everyone who loves has been born of God and knows God. Whoever does not love does not know God, because God is love" (1 John 4:7–8). Love should characterize our doctrine. It is as Francis Schaeffer said: "Biblical orthodoxy without compassion is surely the ugliest thing in the world."[2]

To avoid the trap of condescending Christianity, we need a methodology for discerning between essential orthodox doctrines of the faith—the creeds and the historic conduct of those who held to the creeds—and the God-given freedom to practice Christianity diversely. Dr. Albert Mohler presents a method called "theological triage" that is immensely helpful for this purpose.[3]

Steps of Theological Triage

Theological triage is a method for narrowing down the theological problem we're facing and running it through analytical steps to discern what level of theological importance the issue is: false teaching, heresy, or just a difference of practice.

First-Order Issues

There are three tiers to consider. First-order issues are doctrines essential to the Christian faith (the truths summed up in the creeds):

- the nature of the Trinity
- the physical life, death, and resurrection of Christ
- the hope of eternity
- the final judgment of sin

In addition, we can look to passages such as Acts 15 for the essential behaviors of Christians who held to these truths. Acts 15 in particular emphasizes:

- sanctity of worship (no other gods);
- sanctity of life (honor for the image bearer); and
- sanctity of sex (sexual morality as held by Christ, who affirmed the sexual ethic of Mosaic Law. According to the Jewish ethic upheld by Jesus [Mark 10; Matthew 5:18], all sexual relationships outside of covenant marriage between a man and woman constitute adultery. This includes

premarital or extramarital sex, homosexual unions, pedophilia, and bestiality).

Second-Order Issues

Second-order issues are denominational differences that may prevent fellowship under the same roof. Examples of issues in this category are:

- how to practice baptism;
- how to practice Communion;
- different views of spiritual gifts;
- women in church leadership positions; and
- different views of how salvation works (soteriology).

If you believe in infant baptism, you're probably not going to go to a Baptist church. If you believe that spiritual gifts are for today, and you speak in tongues, you're probably not going to go to a Reformed church. These churches tend to have a specific view on these things that prevents fellowship with those who do not hold that view.

Differing on secondary issues doesn't mean Christians can't be friends, but it means you're probably not going to submit to a church structure that holds a different view than you. This is the primary level of doctrine that separates churches even though they unite around the first-tier, or core, doctrines.

Third-Order Issues

Third-order issues are disagreements that still allow for close fellowship within one church body. Examples of issues in this category are:

- different views of the end times (eschatology);
- perspectives on marriage and parenting;

- personal convictions about modesty and dress;
- convictions about alcohol; and
- personal preferences for music, movies, and other media.

You may have different views on these issues than some people in your church—in fact, you likely do! Third-tier issues grant freedom for diverse thought and Spirit-led conviction.

As we learn to think theologically and dive even deeper into the truths of our faith, we will be doing so in community. And there will always be potential for extremes and error on both sides of the theological spectrum, whether conservative or progressive. Albert Mohler described how these two extremes can look, in terms of theological triage:

> The error of theological liberalism is evident in a basic disrespect for biblical authority and the church's treasury of truth. The mark of true liberalism is the refusal to admit that first-order theological issues even exist. Progressive Christianity treats first-order doctrines as if they were merely third order in importance, and doctrinal ambiguity as the inevitable result. Fundamentalism, on the other hand, tends toward the opposite error. The misjudgment of the true fundamentalist is the belief that all disagreements concern first-order doctrines. Thus, third-order issues are raised to a first order importance, and Christians are wrongly and harmfully divided.[4]

None of us want to contribute to "wrongly and harmfully" dividing Christians, so we must be on guard against elevating third-order issues to first-order importance. Yes, let's help the church adhere to truth, but let's make sure the "truth" we're sharing is both loving and accurate. The Holy Spirit is always at work in His people. He does not need an assistant!

If you are led to speak up about an issue or teacher, start by spending time in prayer. Listen to the Lord's voice. Run it through theological triage. *Then* speak. God is sovereign enough to defend Himself, and He does not need a theological bulldog. He can accomplish more through your educated grace than you can accomplish through unrighteous anger.

The Threat "Out There"

As you close this book and enter your community, my prayer is for you to go out equipped with grace and truth. May the truth be readily on your tongue yet guarded by grace. May we be as Paul told the Ephesian church:

> We will no longer be infants, tossed back and forth by the waves, and blown here and there by every wind of teaching and by the cunning and craftiness of people in their deceitful scheming. Instead, speaking the truth in love, we will grow to become in every respect the mature body of him who is the head, that is, Christ. (4:14–15)

God desires that we know Him truly and accurately. But He also desires for us to present Him to others graciously, because He is the very nature of grace. There is no such thing as a *prideful* biblical theology. Let's not pretend there is.

The truth of God is what this culture needs, and it needs that truth from you. Yes, you! You are particularly equipped to share your faith with the people God saw fit to put in your corner of the world. I don't have your coworkers. I don't have your extended family. You do.

It can be tempting to view our anti-Christ culture as a threat— the threat "out there" as Christians gather "in here" for support. Christians should be supported (that's what the church is for!), but viewing the culture as a threat makes it very difficult to love people within it. Let us reframe our view. What if we looked at the world the way Jesus looked at the crowds as He was coming to Jerusalem? "Jerusalem, Jerusalem, you who kill the prophets and stone those sent to you, how often I have longed to gather your children together, as a hen gathers her chicks under her wings, and you were not willing" (Matthew 23:37).

Only four chapters later, Jerusalem killed Jesus. He knew the sins of the people. He knew the evil, the pain, and the sorrow to come. Yet when He looked at them, He saw helpless chicks. He saw people God longed to welcome home. Until the very end of His life on earth, Jesus loved people enough to tell them the best news: *God longs to dwell with you. Just say yes to Him. Believe in God, believe also in Me.*

Students of the Heart of God

The study of theology equips us to love well. If it doesn't, it's not a biblical theology. The heart of all this truth about God throbs with the rhythm of endless grace. No one is too far gone to turn around and run home. The arms of Christ were pinned to a cross once for all time, and they remain open to all who will call upon His name.

Theology invites us to know that story so well it becomes a part of us, and as we live our ordinary lives of grocery runs and school drop-off and data entry and night classes, it spills out of us as *hope*. Hope to be known. Hope to be loved. Hope that God doesn't give up on us but actually moved heaven and earth to dwell with us.

Doctrine leads to devotion, attention to adoration. We get to spend every day of life in Christ learning more about who He is and how He loves. Isn't that exciting? We *get* to be students of God's heart. We get to be part of a bigger story, one that began long before our existence yet took into account our existence. God is leading us further up and further in[5] to an experience of Him, one that is deeper than we've ever known. It is amazing, really, how diving into the truths about Jesus incites a closeness even the best devotional can sometimes miss.

I hope this book is just the first step on a long road of theological exploration. I hope you are inspired to be a student, not just today or tomorrow but for all of your life. You are a theologian now—and there's no going back!

Acknowledgments

This book would not exist without the wisdom, input, and support of the community I'm in. I would first like to thank the team at W Publishing—Stephanie Newton, Carrie Marrs, and freelance editor Sam O'Neal, who refined the words and theology of this book. I believe theological pushback makes for better ideas in a clearer voice, and that's what *Every Woman a Theologian* needed.

To Joel Muddamalle, Jeremy Jenkins, Ryan Coatney, Johnny Whitcomb, and Josh Nadeau, my brothers and co-laborers in Christ: thank you for supporting this work and inspiring me through your own.

To the women who have prayed for me, carried me, and led me closer to Christ through this process: Lisa J., Lisa H., Courtney, Hali, Autumn, Tiffany, Diana, Laura, Hunter, September, and so many more. You are as much a part of this ministry as I am, and I praise God upon every thought of you.

To my family, who makes sure I walk the walk and don't just talk the talk—ha!: thank you for giving me the foundation and education to reach many with the gospel of Christ. I love you!

And to Josh, who cared for babies, reminded me of deadlines, walked with me through the writing, and has made every good work of mine possible: thank you.

> You were not too much a man to fold towels,
> Bravely unthreatened by a wife
> Made public, visible, in a world not your own—
> So you made it your world too.

Notes

Introduction

1. C. S. Lewis, *Mere Christianity* (New York: HarperCollins, 1998), 54.
2. Athanasius, Penelope Lawson, and C. S. Lewis, *On The Incarnation* (England, 1944), 9.
3. See Peter Harrison, "Christianity and the Rise of Western Science," *ABC Religion & Ethics*, May 8, 2012, https://www.abc.net.au/religion /christianity-and-the-rise-of-western-science/10100570.
4. John Shook, "Timeline of American Thought," American Institute for Philosophical and Cultural Thought, accessed June 23, 2022, http:// americanphilosophy.net/timeline-of-american-thought.
5. "In U.S., Decline of Christianity Continues at Rapid Pace," Pew Research Center, October 17, 2019, https://www.pewforum.org/2019/10/17/in-u-s -decline-of-christianity-continues-at-rapid-pace/.
6. G. K. Chesterton, *St. Thomas Aquinas* (Mineola: Dover Publications, 2009), 11.

Chapter 1

1. Terry Noble, "Do We Still Need the Old Testament Now that We Have the New Testament?", *Christianity Today*, December 11, 2012, https://www .christianitytoday.com/biblestudies/bible-answers/theology/do-we-still -need-old-testament.html.
2. W. A. Criswell, *The Scarlet Thread Through the Bible* (Nashville: Lifeway Press, 2014) https://gospelproject.lifeway.com/wp-content/uploads /tgp2018/2018/04/The-Scarlet-Thread-Criswell.pdf.

3. *Merriam-Webster Dictionary*, s.v. "canon," accessed June 23, 2022, https://www.merriam-webster.com/dictionary/canon.

4. Christopher Rollston, "Who Wrote the Torah According to the Torah?", Thetorah.com, 2017, https://www.thetorah.com/article/who-wrote-the-torah-according-to-the-torah.

5. Timothy Paul Jones, *How We Got the Bible* (Peabody: Rose Publishing, 2015), 53.

6. Bill Warren and Archie W. England, "Bible Formation and the Canon," *Holman Illustrated Bible Dictionary*, ed., Charles Draper, et al. www.mystudybible.com.

7. Christopher L. Scott, "Bibliology: The Bible As the Ultimate Authority," *Christopher L. Scott* (blog), February 12, 2018, https://christopherscottblog.com/bibliology-bible-ultimate-authority/.

8. Don Stewart, "What About the Mistakes in the Various Copies of the Bible?", *Blue Letter Bible*, accessed January 25, 2022, https://www.blueletterbible.org/Comm/stewart_don/faq/bible-difficulties/question25-what-about-mistakes-in-copies-of-the-bible.cfm.

9. Mark Water, ed., *The New Encyclopedia of Christian Quotations* (Ada, MI: Baker Books, 2000), 119.

10. Andrena Sawyer (@andrena_sawyer), "We can't weaponize Scripture when it defends our behavior and reject it when it convicts us," Twitter.

11. C. S. Lewis, *The Weight of Glory: And Other Addresses* (NY: HarperCollins, 1949), 140.

Chapter 2

1. Michael Reeves, *Delighting in the Trinity* (Westmont: IVP, 2012), 16.

2. John Behr, "One God Father Almighty," *Modern Theology* 34, no. 3 (July 2018), https://frjohnbehr.com/wp-content/uploads/2019/07/Behr-One_God_Father_Almighty.pdf.

3. Reeves, *Delighting in the Trinity*.

4. John Oswalt, *The Bible Among the Myths* (Grand Rapids, MI: Zondervan, 2009), 71.

5. George Eldon Ladd, *A Theology of the New Testament* (Grand Rapids, MI: Eerdmans Publishing, 1993), 81.

6. Aaron Armstrong, "Why Do We Say That God Is Holy?" The Gospel Project, December 4, 2019, https://gospelproject.lifeway.com/god-holy/.

7. R.C. Sproul, *The Holiness of God* (Sanford, FL: Ligonier Ministries, 2006), 31.

8. Tim Keller, "Justice in the Bible," *Life in the Gospel*, Fall 2020, https://quarterly.gospelinlife.com/justice-in-the-bible/.

9. Keller, "Justice in the Bible."

10. Wayne Grudem, *Systematic Theology* (Grand Rapids, MI: Zondervan, 1994), 216.

Chapter 3

1. Hans Halvorson and Helge Kragh, "Cosmology and Theology," *Stanford Encyclopedia of Philosophy*, Winter 2021, https://plato.stanford.edu /entries/cosmology-theology/#8.

2. "What Is Living Cosmology?", Got Questions, accessed June 23, 2022, https://www.gotquestions.org/living-cosmology.html.

3. C. S. Lewis, *The Magician's Nephew* (London: HarperCollins Publishers, 2009), 113.

4. Lewis, *The Magician's Nephew*, 117.

5. Anthony Briggman, "Irenaeus: Creation & the Father's Two Hands," Henry Center for Theological Understanding, April 19, 2017, https:// henrycenter.tiu.edu/2017/04/irenaeus-creation-the-fathers-two-hands/.

6. Athanasius, "Chapter 1: Creation and the Fall," *Blue Letter Bible*, https:// www.blueletterbible.org/Comm/athanasius/Incarnation/Creation_and_the _Fall.cfm.

7. Michael Heiser, "Genesis 1:2 and the 'Gap Theory,'" *Dr. Michael S. Heiser* (blog), September 28, 2010, https://drmsh.com/genesis-12-and-the-gap -theory/.

8. Mildred Bangs Wynkoop, *Foundations of Wesleyan-Arminian Theology* (Kansas City, MO: Beacon Hill Press, 2007), 100–101.

9. Craig S. Keener, *The IVP Bible Background Commentary* (Downers Grove, IL: IVP Academic, 2014).

10. Carl F. Henry, *Basic Christian Doctrines* (Grand Rapids, MI: Baker Book House, 1979), 105.

11. Henry, *Basic Christian Doctrines*, 104.

12. John Wesley, "Sermon 85. On Working Out Our Own Salvation," Sermon 85. on Working Out Our Own Salvation, accessed November 16, 2022, https://wesleyworks.smu.edu/exist/apps/srophe/sermons/85.

13. Joseph Stump, *The Christian Faith: A System of Christian Dogmatics* (Philadelphia: Muhlenberg Press, 1942), 115.

14. John Piper, "What Is the Meaning of Life?" Desiring God, February 19, 2021, https://www.desiringgod.org/interviews/what-is-the-meaning-of-life.

15. Bertrand Russell, *A Free Man's Worship* (Portland, ME: T.B. Mosher, 1923), 6–7.

16. John Milton, "Paradise Lost, Book IV," https://poets.org/poem/paradise -lost-book-iv-argument.

17. Michael S. Heiser, *The Unseen Realm: Recovering the Supernatural World View of the Bible* (Bellingham, WA: Lexham Press, 2015), 104.

18. D. Thomas Lancaster, *Unrolling the Scroll* (Marshfield, MO: First Fruits of Zion, 2014), 9.

Chapter 4

1. "What a Friend We Have in Jesus," Joseph Medlicott Scriven (1855), accessed October 16, 2022, https://hymnary.org/text/what_a_friend _we_have_in_jesus_all_our_s.

2. Cory Mansfield, "The Ultimate Guide to Old Testament Prophecies Jesus Christ Fulfilled," Preaching.com, accessed October 16, 2022, https://www.preaching.com/articles/the-ultimate-guide-to-old-testament -prophecies-jesus-christ-fulfilled/.

3. David Jeremiah, "The Principle of Double Fulfillment in Interpreting Prophecy," accessed June 23, 2022, https://biblicalstudies.org.uk/pdf/grace -journal/13-2_13.pdf.

4. Jeremiah, "The Principle of Double Fulfillment."

5. "How Many Prophecies Did Jesus Fulfill?" Got Questions, accessed June 23, 2022, https://www.gotquestions.org/prophecies-of-Jesus.html.

6. Douglas McCready, "He Came Down from Heaven: The Preexistence of Christ Revisited," *JETS* 40, no. 3 (September 1997): 419–32, https://www .etsjets.org/files/JETS-PDFs/40/40-3/40-3-pp419-432_JETS.pdf.

7. McCready, "He Came Down from Heaven."

8. St. Athanasius, *On The Incarnation*, 17–18.

9. "The Apostles' Creed," The Church of England, accessed October 16, 2022, https://www.churchofengland.org/our-faith/what-we-believe/apostles -creed.

10. "Docetism," *Encyclopedia Britannica,* April 11, 2014, https://www .britannica.com/topic/Docetism.

11. Carl F. Henry, *Basic Christian Doctrines* (Grand Rapids, MI: Baker Book House, 1979), 125.

12. J. Warner Wallace, "Jesus Specifically Said, 'I Am God,'" Cold Case Christianity, November 7, 2016, https://coldcasechristianity.com/writings /jesus-specifically-said-i-am-god/.

13. Joseph Stump, *The Christian Faith: A System of Christian Dogmatics* (Philadelphia: Muhlenberg Press, 1942), 129.

14. Henry, *Basic Christian Doctrines*, 153.

15. Henry, *Basic Christian Doctrines*, 153.

16. George Eldon Ladd, *A Theology of the New Testament* (Grand Rapids, MI: Eerdmans, 1993), 466–77.

17. "The Language of Law in Paul," Bible.org, accessed June 23, 2022, https://bible.org/article/language-law-paul.
18. Marianne Meye Thompson, "Christus Victor: The Salvation of God and the Cross of Christ," Fuller Studio, https://fullerstudio.fuller.edu/christus-victor-the-salvation-of-god-and-the-cross-of-christ/.
19. Thompson, "Christus Victor."
20. Wayne Grudem, *Systematic Theology* (Grand Rapids, MI: Zondervan, 1994), 580.
21. Grudem, *Systematic Theology*, 580.
22. N. T. Wright, *When God Became King* (San Francisco: HarperOne, 2016), 207.
23. Alan Richardson, *An Introduction to the Theology of the New Testament*, 1958, Harper & Row Publishers p. 197
24. Henry, *Basic Christian Doctrines*, 141–42.
25. Gary R. Habermas, "Jesus' Resurrection: When Truth Confronts Our Worst Suffering," 2007, https://www.garyhabermas.com/articles/tc_devotional/whentruthconfrontssuffering.htm.

Chapter 5

1. George Long, "Manumissio," quoted in William Smith, *A Dictionary of Greek and Roman Antiquities* (1875), 730–31, https://penelope.uchicago.edu/Thayer/E/Roman/Texts/secondary/SMIGRA*/Manumissio.html.
2. Matthew Bates, *Salvation by Allegiance Alone* (Grand Rapids, MI: Baker, 2017), 82.
3. Handley Carr Glyn Moule, *Outlines of Christian Doctrine* (London: Hodder and Stoughton, 1890), 76, https://archive.org/details/outlineschristi01moulgoog/page/n76/mode/2up.
4. Bishop Moule, "Justification by Faith," *The Fundamental Doctrines of the Christian Faith*, ed. R.A. Torrey (New York: George H. Doran Company, 1918).
5. S. Lewis Johnson, "The Fundamental Principle of Justification," SLJ Institute, accessed October 17, 2022, https://sljinstitute.net/the-theology-of-the-reformers/the-fundamental-principle-of-justification/.
6. Anthony Maas, "Salvation," *The Catholic Encyclopedia Vol. 13*, 1912, https://www.newadvent.org/cathen/13407a.htm.
7. Johann Peter Kirsch, "Council of Trent," *The Catholic Encyclopedia Vol. 15*, 1912, https://www.newadvent.org/cathen/15030c.htm.
8. Dennis Bratcher, ed., "The Confession of Dositheus," CRI/Voice, 2018, http://www.crivoice.org/creeddositheus.html.
9. Justin Perdue, "Are Calvinism and Reformed Theology the Same Thing?"

Theocast, July 6, 2020, https://theocast.org/are-calvinism-and-reformed -theology-the-same-thing/.

10. "Jacobus Arminius," *Encyclopedia Britannica*, 2021, https://www .britannica.com/biography/Jacobus-Arminius.

11. Dutch Mennonnite Conference, "The Dordrecht Confession of Faith," 1632, https://www.nobts.edu/baptist-center-theology/confessions /Dordrecht_Confession_of_Faith.pdf.

12. Mark S.J. Bosco, "Ite Inflammate Omnia: Setting the World on Fire with Learning," Conversations on Jesuit Higher Education: Vol. 49, Article 3 (2016).

13. "Jefferson's Letter to the Danbury Baptists," Library of Congress, January 1, 1802, https://www.loc.gov/loc/lcib/9806/danpre.html.

Chapter 6

1. Martin Manser, ed., "3010, God, the Holy Spirit," *Dictionary of Bible Themes*, 2009, https://www.biblegateway.com/resources/dictionary -of-bible-themes/3010-God-Holy-Spirit.

2. Kenneth Berding, "What Is the Unforgivable Sin? What Is Blasphemy Against the Spirit?", *The Good Book* (blog), Biola University, February 3, 2021, https://www.biola.edu/blogs/good-book-blog/2021/what-is-the -unforgiveable-sin-what-is-blasphemy-against-the-spirit.

3. Dwight L. Moody, *Secret Power* (New Kensington, PA: Bridge-Logos Inc, 2013), 32.

4. Jennifer Anne Cox, "New Testament Prophecy and Its Implication for the Ministry of Women," Feminist Theology 25, no. 1 (August 11, 2016): 29–40, https://doi.org/10.1177/0966735016657705.

5. Anthony Thiselton, *The First Epistle to the Corinthians* (Grand Rapids, MI: Eerdmans, 2013), 826.

Chapter 7

1. Oswald Chambers, *If Ye Shall Ask* (London: Simpkin Marshall, 1941), 12.

2. George Eldon Ladd, *A Theology of the New Testament* (Grand Rapids, MI: Eerdmans, 1974), 582.

3. F. F. Bruce, *The New International Commentary on the New Testament: Acts* (Grand Rapids, MI: Eerdmans, 1988), 73.

4. Stephen Binz, *Church of the Holy Spirit: Part 1: Acts of the Apostles* (New London, CT: Twenty-Third Publications, 2013), 26.

5. Binz, *Church of the Holy Spirit*, 26.

6. Freddy Cardoza, "Understanding Biblical Christian Fellowship," Grace Theological Seminary, March 17, 2021, https://seminary.grace.edu /understanding-biblical-christian-fellowship/.

7. Mark Ross, "In Essentials Unity, in Non-Essentials Liberty, in All Things Charity," Ligonier Ministries, September 1, 2009, https://www.ligonier.org/learn/articles/essentials-unity-non-essentials-liberty-all-things.

8. "General Council of Trent: Seventh Session: Council Fathers - 1547" Papal Encyclicals Online, last updated February 20, 2020, https://www.papalencyclicals.net/councils/trent/seventh-session.htm.

9. J.H. Thomas, Come, Thou Fount of Every Blessing. Thomas, J. H., Catskill, monographic, 1872. Notated Music. https://www.loc.gov/item/sm1872.04071/.

10. Eric Strattan, "Three Ways to Identify and Address Spiritual Abuse," Cornerstone University, September 26, 2017, https://www.cornerstone.edu/blog-post/three-ways-to-identify-and-address-spiritual-abuse-in-ministry-leadership/.

Chapter 8

1. Miroslav Volf, *Free of Charge: Giving and Forgiving in a Culture Stripped of Grace* (Grand Rapids, MI: Zondervan, 2006), 138–39.

2. William Barclay, *Revelation of John, Vol. II* (Louisville, KY: Westminster John Knox Press, 2017), 20.

Conclusion

1. G. K. Chesterton, *Orthodoxy* (New York: John Lane Company, 1908), 20.

2. Joseph Holden, *Harvest Handbook of Apologetics* (Eugene, OR: Harvest House Publishers, 2018), 74.

3. Albert Mohler, "A Call for Theological Triage and Christian Maturity," The Southern Baptist Theological Seminary, July 12, 2005, https://albertmohler.com/2005/07/12/a-call-for-theological-triage-and-christian-maturity.

4. Mohler, "A Call for Theological Triage."

5. C. S. Lewis, *The Last Battle* (New York: Harper Collins, 1994).

About the Author

Phylicia Masonheimer is a bestselling author, Bible teacher, and host of the *Verity* podcast. She is the founder of Every Woman a Theologian, an organization teaching Christians how to know what they believe, why they believe it, and how to live their faith authentically in the world. Phylicia loves good books, black coffee, goats, and gardening. She lives on a northern Michigan farm with her husband, Josh, and their three children: Adeline, Geneva, and Ivan.

Here's a sneak peek at the accompanying

Every Woman a *Theologian*

COMPANION WORKBOOK

INTRODUCTION AND BIBLIOLOGY

The Very Breath of God

KNOW WHAT
YOU BELIEVE.

LIVE IT
CONFIDENTLY.

COMMUNICATE
IT GRACIOUSLY.

INTRODUCTION
AND BIBLIOLOGY

Just a reminder: the exercises below are based on the introduction and chapter one: Bibliology in *Every Woman a Theologian (or EWAT)*.

Opening Prayer

You did it—you're here! Begin your time of study by taking this verse to prayer: "... so is my [the Lord's] word that goes out from my mouth: It will not return to me empty, but will accomplish what I desire and achieve the purpose for which I sent it." (Isaiah 55:11)

Write a few lines of prayer thanking God for this truth and asking that His purposes would be accomplished in you.

_____

_____

_____

_____

_____

_____

Vocabulary Review

The basics—they really do matter! Let's start by defining our terms, which are all found in definition boxes in chapter one of the book. The best way to learn these definitions is to write them out one more time.

Theology: _____

Humanism: _____

Bibliology: _____

Canon: _____

Genre: _____

Know What You Believe

How to Use a Bible Commentary

Have you ever read a Bible passage and then thought to yourself, "What in the world was that about?"

Don't worry. You're not the only one. Take your confusion as an encouraging sign of two things: one, you are actually paying attention, and two, you're not letting your own assumptions fill in the holes. But you don't have to live in confusion. Take a moment to consult a Bible dictionary or concordance—or maybe both! These books are typically heavy reference books with teeny, tiny font. Don't let that intimidate you. These books are *for you*. Also, there are amazing dictionary and concordance resources online, so you don't have to worry about the font size anymore!

The purpose of these two types of books is to provide context for the Bible passages that you're reading. They'll give you more information that hopefully will help shed some light on God's word. Bible dictionaries give historical context and Bible concordances give literary context. My favorites are *Strong's Exhaustive Concordance* and *Zondervan Bible Dictionary.*

Any good Bible dictionary will provide you with maps, pictures, and in-depth descriptions. It turns out that knowing something about warfare in ancient times will help you read the biblical books of history with more understanding and appreciation.

A concordance will help you look deeply at the meaning of the particular words in the passage. It will offer cross-references, or other verses that use the same word, to help you understand the meaning of that word in that passage. A concordance is an extremely helpful resource if you're trying to understand the author's original intent with their book, letter, or poem.

Just remember that these dictionaries and concordances are for anyone who wants to understand the Bible with more comprehensive context—these tools are for you. Use them!

Head Knowledge

Let's explore our terms and talk about your own experiences. I'm interested in where you are—both right now and where you've been before.

What's your personal reaction to being called a "theologian"? Does that title fit you? Why or why not?

Where do theologians begin? Look near the end of the chapter.

Take a moment to remember a time you defended your faith. What was the circumstance (speaking to a fellow believer, or non-believer, or someone whom you did not know their perspective)? How did that feel? How were you received? What went well and what perhaps could have been improved upon?

Consider the different genres of the Bible. Which genre appeals to you the most? The least? Which genre do you want to know more about?

....

....

....

Heart Change

It's time to dig deeper. Read through all of these questions before you get started. Start with the one that appeals to you the most. You're wrestling, not answering questions on a test. Start with the question that has a meaningful link into your day-to-day experiences. You'll know it when you see it.

The Bible was not received as a one-time revelation, but in multiple books across both eras and genres. What aspects does Scripture gain because of the way that it was developed?

....

....

....

....

....

....

....

The Bible is the *kanon* (or measure) that informs everything else about us; for example, political beliefs, identity, and sexuality. Why do you think that this standard is so often "flipped," i.e., identity informing the interpretation of Scripture?

What's the difference between plenary and verbal inspiration?

Theologian's Questions

What unanswered questions do you have about theology? What piqued your curiosity in this chapter? What caused confusion? Write these questions down so you can find out more by asking them to other believers or pursuing them in further research.

Common Ground

These questions are written for group discussion, but they can be used in individual study or as conversation starters. As we travel from head knowledge to heart change, we start reaching out toward others in conversation, searching for common ground.

Everyone, whether they know it or not, is walking around with a theology. What contributes to a person's theological formation— what influences why a person believes what they believe?

_____

_____

_____

How was Scripture received during the time it was written? In other words, who received these words and how did they receive it? How long was it before the words of Scripture were considered inspired?

_____

_____

_____

What is the significance of the discovery of the Dead Sea Scrolls?

_____

_____

_____

_____

Scripture is infallible, that is, unable to deceive, but teachers are not. What kinds of accountability measures do we need to have in place for the people who teach us Scripture? What are some of the signs exhibited by good teachers—how can we recognize who they are?

_____

_____

_____

The Bible says that morality is not subjective. This has always been difficult for the world to accept. We've been trying to determine our own rules since the beginning. Often, conversations about this can be paralyzed by conflicting emotions from both sides. Look again at Phy's conversation in the introduction. How did she lead into her differing opinion? How can we discuss the idea of objective morality with a hostile culture?

_____

_____

_____

For the Christian, what is the purpose of the Bible?

_____

_____

_____

Live It Boldly

So . . . what are you going to DO about it?

The Bible is God's word given to us. It is alive and living. In a very real way, the Bible is God's voice. So, where is your Bible? Not right now. I mean, right now, it's probably on your lap or table or the arm of your chair. Where do you usually keep it? Could you keep it in a place that reminded you to use it more often?

We have the opportunity to hear the voice of God every single day, if only we are willing to open up the Bible. Consider practical and realistic ways you want to incorporate God's voice into your daily life. Write them here, not as mere goals, but promises to yourself to get to know God more deeply and intimately over the course of the next eight weeks.

_____

_____

_____

_____

_____

Moving Forward

What worked well for you this week?

_____

_____

_____

What obstacles did you have to overcome?

_____

_____

_____

Where can you see some walls coming down?

_____

_____

_____

What is one thing of praise you received this week or learned that brought freedom or joy?

_____

_____

Thanksgiving

God, your character is the canon by which all truth is measured.
Your Word does not return to you empty. Thank You for the work
Your Word is already doing in my life. Help me to look to You as
I lift up these requests to you. Remind me to be grateful for the
graces and blessings You've poured out on me.

Scan this QR code for a free summary video from Phy!